TIBETAN ART

TIBETAN ART

Lokesh Chandra

KONECKY & KONECKY

Konecky & Konecky
72 Ayers Point Road
Old Saybrook, CT 06475

Please visit us on the web: www.koneckyandkonecky.com

This edition published by special arrangement with Niyogi Books.

Designed by: Arati Subramanyam
Navidita Thapa
Cover Design: Cindy Labreacht

ISBN: 1-56852-761-6

Printed in India

CONTENTS

Preface

Unto the Mindground of Tibetan Art

Even as the Sun ripens the corn and the fruits of the earth, so do the Buddhas, the Enlightened Ones, emit upon *saṁsāra* the radiances of their all-embracing Wisdom and Compassion, fuelling the growth and maturity of the bodhic essence implanted in all living beings. In course of time, the human Śākyamuni Buddha became a symbol. *Nirvāṇa* was transformed into paradise, and *karma* became modifiable by prayer. Elaborate patterns emerged. With metaphysical daring, this Eternal *par excellence,* definable by negatives alone, became the bejewelled *sambhoga-kāya,* passionately embracing his transcendental consort *(prajñā).* Extreme serenity was identified with extreme passion, crystal light with the fire of love, the intangible with the intoxication of the senses. Sensuality and symbolism, metaphysical filigree of jewels, the earth and sky were celebrated in *thaṅka*s, images, *maṇḍala*s, and in depictions of *siddha*s and saints. Hymns incarnated into scrolls and statues to carry eternal depths to the eyes of the faithful of the earth.

In Tibet, iconographic art became the frozen music of forms, the breath of statues, the stillness of painted scrolls, and the flowing rhythms of her eternal quest. The irradiation of her wisdom and mystery, the feel of her shadows and the voices of her spaces, her crystallized grandeur in the brilliant syndrome of form constitute the heart of her culture.

Tibetan art is the pictorial awareness of inner experiences in a pilgrimage to the timeless omnipresence of cosmic consciousness. It is a purified meditative universe to transform our environment into poise and serenity.

> Who speaks the sound of an echo?
> Who paints the image in a mirror?
> Where are the spectacles in a dream?
> Nowhere at all—
> That's the nature of the mind.
>
> —*Citta-guhya-dohā*
> *(Derge Tanjur 2443 folio 70)*

The most characteristic product of Tibetan pictorial art is the *thaṅka,* found in temples and private chapels. They are carried in religious processions, and often serve to illustrate a sermon.

Let us visit the studio of a Tibetan artist. Usually a Lama, he is versed in sacred lore and accompanies his work by a continuous recitation of prayers. The holy Kanjur prescribes that he must be a sacred person of good conduct, learned in the scriptures, and reserved in his manners. The saintly image can be painted only in a clean place, and therefore, the studio of an artist is always spic and span. The artist usually sits on the ground holding the painting on his knees. Around him are his disciples who prepare colours and attend to the various needs of their master. An advanced student can help in colouring the outlines of figures drawn by the master. The paintings are usually on silk or linen, stretched on a frame. After stretching the fabric, it is covered with a thick mixture of glue and chalk, which is then polished with the smooth surface of a conch. Once this is done, the outlines of the figures are drawn with red or black ink.

The work is carried out meticulously, so that minute details of the ornamentation are attended to before colouration. A mistake in the measurements of a body, given in the iconographic manuals, is a cardinal sin. Sometimes, another Lama reads prayers while the artist is at work. An intense spiritual atmosphere envelopes the creation of a painting.

The face of a Buddha or Bodhisattva is preferably drawn on an auspicious date. The full moon *(pūrṇimā)* and new moon *(amāvasyā)* of every month are sacred in Tibet. The artist draws the features of the faces on the full moon day, and colours them on the new moon day.

When the artist has completed his work, a consecration ceremony makes it the habitation of the deity and of his/her entourage. The ceremony is called *sādhana* (Tibetan: sgrub-byed). The officiant purifies himself for the rite. Holy water is sanctified through a long process; two vessels are used: one in the inner circle of the altar, and the other on the lower and outer platform of the altar. The inner pot is called rnam-rgyal bum-pa *(vijaya-kalaśa)*, and the outer one, las-thams-cad-paḥi bum-pa *(karma-kalaśa)*. In accordance with the methods of *yoga*, the *iṣṭadevatā* or tutelary deity who dwells in the heart-lotus is transferred to the nostrils by *prāṇāyāma* through the internal channels. Through the medium of a flower, the deity is brought over to the jar in the centre of the ritual vessels. The arrangement of these vessels corresponds to the situation of the heart-lotus, the abode of the deity. The water in the jar is thus sanctified and may now be sprinkled on any object except on a *thaṅka* as it would ruin the painting. Instead a mirror is held up, and the holy water sprinkled on the reflection of the painting . The *thaṅka* is now sacrosanct.

In the recesses of Tibet's sancta, the images, now peaceful, now terrific, come alive before the eyes, and engrave themselves deep into the consciousness. They seem to float out of the walls and take possession of us. They are visions evoked with primordial forces, conjured up by painters by their wizardry of living forces. Alongside the smiling Buddha, suggesting unruffled peace and triumph over the conflicting opposites of life, is the sneer of demons reflecting the senseless turmoil of the human subconscious.

Tibetan art is closely connected with ritual and meditation. Nobody sets hands to it who has not attuned himself to the divine worlds he wants to represent according to traditional symbols. *Na adevo devam arcayet* (One should worship after becoming divinized). The image does not spring from fancy, but accords to carefully laid out prescriptions of proportions, attributes, colours, and the chanting of *mantras*. It is the abode of a deity, inhabiting the liturgic force.

Tantras developed from the mysterious orgies of the dark jungles of India to the ideal form as the Logos *(Dharma-kāya),* as perceptible perfection *(sambhoga-kāya),* and as the phenomenal body *(nirmāṇa-kāya).* In the amorous embrace of the *Yab-Yum* deities, the male deity represents compassion *(karuṇā),* while the female deity stands for wisdom *(prajñā),* signifying a lightning intuition of the Truth, united with the altruistic force of compassion. The serene and terrifying aspects of deities are to combat and overcome the forces of evil. Extreme serenity and extreme passion, the most abstract defined by the most carnal, the invisible and intangible in the intoxication of the senses: it is the oneness of the mind of the universe and of the divine in the living non-duality of the basest and the noblest. The body itself is a divine mansion *(maṇḍala).* The *Yoginī Niguma* says:

> The divine male and divine female unite ...
> Spiritual ecstasy increases;
> The elixir of union, blue in colour,
> Fills the body from the heart downward, ...
> Purifying causes of misery and mental defilements.

The *Yab-Yum* figures of the *Inner Tantras* represent the complex thought of Esoteric Buddhism. They have no sexual connotation. At the highest level, every samsaric manifestation turns into a symbol. The *Yab-Yum* deities culminate in the identification of the meditator with the Divine. The *Atiyoga* scriptures explain as follows: The *Yab,* 'Father', is the means *(upāya),* the *māyā*-body, which gradually adapts to voidness and is transformed into the consciousness of Being. The *Yum,* 'Mother', embracing the 'Father', represents higher cognition. The *Yab-Yum* symbol is a visual support to the processes of evocation and meditation. It is an imagery to lead to heights of contemplations, visions of a lofty philosophical experience, a symbolic concretisation of the Divine. The iconic *(sākāra)* is to conjure the aniconic *(nirākāra);* we have to 'read' or 'visualise' the iconography. We have to go beyond physical 'seeing' to the metaphysical 'visualisation' in the expansion of the Consciousness. *Yab-Yum* are thus the 'Divine Parents of Transcendence.'

The *maṇḍala* delineates a consecrated superfice and protects it from disintegrating forces. The mystic stands in the centre and identifies himself with the forces that govern the universe. The *maṇḍala* is born of an interior impulse to become a support for meditation. It is the mysterious intrinsic necessity of the human spirit.

*Tantra*s summon us to ensphere ourselves in the heart of Divinised Humanity, wherein we perceive the fusion of the Eternal Spirit, the earth, the sky, and the stars, in the intense pilgrimage of living, where the body and the spiritual self are one, where purity and orgy are fragments of life and liberation.

Tibetan prototypes go back to the 7th century when Nepalese artists worked at the court of King Sroṅ-btsan-sgam-po, or Khotanese artists during the reign of Khri Gtsug-lde-btsan (AD 755-797), or Dhīman and his son Bitpāla of Nalanda in the 8th-9th century. Influences of South India in Tibetan art are indicated by Sum-pa-mkhan-po. During the 10th century and later, Kashmiri artists painted and sculpted at Tabo, Tholing, Tsaparang and elsewhere. The Sa-skya monastery had Kashmiri images. Nepalese artists like Prince Aniko were at the Mongol court on the advice of Phagspa, the Imperial Preceptor. They were a ubiquitous presence in Tibet, the Hsi-hsia kingdom, China, Mongolia, Buryatia and other Lamaist lands.

Divine forms do not remain in distant heavens but descend into us: I am the cosmos and the Buddhas are in me. Iconic representations transform into aniconic awareness. The creative play of colour values scintillates into luminosities of deeper meaning. In a state of composure, light rays of pristine cognitions burst forth in a steady flow or in a furious blaze, as the '*Tantra* of the Secret Heart' *(Gsaṅ-sñiṅ)* says:

> An all-encompassing configuration
> Having neither periphery nor centre
> Surpasses all thought and just is.

Tibetan art *is* renaissance. The resplendent colours are not really of this world. There is no world, only the Void, the *Śūnya.* The forms are but a shaft from the unknown.

—Lokesh Chandra, Delhi, 2008

Tibet: The Land of Spaces and Silences

Where the Buddha, the Perfect One, could exhort:
'Here, O bhikṣus, are the roots of trees,
Here are empty places: Meditate.'

(Majjhima-nikāya 1.118)

In the lap of the Himalayas nestles Tibet 'the Land of Snows', ensconced in the blue silence of her icy peaks, the ochre silence of her rocks. Once it was honey-combed with monasteries rich with their realizations of esoteric universes. A Tibetan inscription calls her 'divine territory...a land that is a mine of wisdom.'

Buddhism was introduced in Tibet in the 7th century AD during the rule of Sroṅ-btsan-sgam-po who ruled from AD 618-649. The first Buddhist images were brought to Tibet by his Chinese queen Wencheng and also by his Nepalese queen Bhṛikuṭī (Tibetan: Thitsun). Buddhism assimilated local beliefs, spirits and other supernatural convictions. Tibetan kings were '*Dharma* Kings'. The Tibetan empire reached its peak during the reign of Khri Sroṅ-lde-btsan (r. *c.* 755-797). He captured the imperial capital of China Ch'ang-an in AD 763. A devoted Buddhist, the first major monastery was constructed at Samye during his reign. He invited Padmasambhava from India to tame indigenous demons, to introduce meditation techniques and to establish Buddhism on a sound basis. Padmasambhava requested the Tibetan king to invite Śāntarakṣita who introduced the Buddhist Mādhyamika teachings. Both of them supervised the construction of the monastery as a *Sumeru* on the basis of the Odantapuri Monastery in Bihar. It was inaugurated in AD 767, and Buddhism was declared the official religion of Tibet. Śāntarakṣita became the abbot and ordained seven young Tibetan monks. A debate was held at Samye in AD 792 to determine whether the Chinese or the Indian tradition of Buddhism would be followed. In the debate between the Indian Kamalaśīla and the Chinese Hva-shang, the outcome was in favour of Indian Tantrism, which was closer to the Tibetan inclination of the supernatural. Political considerations also tempered the decision not to translate Buddhist *sūtras* from Chinese but from Sanskrit, hence, to develop the Tibetan language on the pattern of Sanskrit. This led to the standardization of Buddhist terminology in the dictionary *Mahāvyutpatti* under an Imperial Commission of *Dharma* under Ral-pa-can in AD 826.

The translation of Buddhist *sūtras* and *tantras* was undertaken in earnest with the help of a standard terminology of Buddhist philosophy: names of the vast pantheon of gods, goddesses, guardian deities, names of the different traditions of philosophers, *siddhas* and other teachers. Over a thousand *sūtras* and *tantras* were translated into

Tibetan and compiled in a corpus termed 'Kanjur'. Kanjur means 'words of the Buddha'. They run into 108 mega-volumes. Extensive commentaries on them by Indian masters, treatises on philosophy, monastic discipline, *jātakas*, epistles, logic, grammar, medicine, lexicons, architecture, painting and sculpture were also translated into Tibetan from Sanskrit. These were collected in 226 volumes of the Tanjur running into over 200,000 pages. Both the Kanjur and Tanjur comprise more than 4,500 works in different traditional xylographed editions. The Tanjur has texts devoted to the making of matrices of votive *stūpas* and images, metallurgy of statues, and principles of painting. The *Citra-lakṣaṇa* of Nagnajit (extant only in its Tibetan rendering) dilates on the metaphors of the eyes:

> The eyes of yogins, bespeaking of equanimity,
> should be made to resemble a bow of bamboo.
> The eyes of women and lovers should resemble
> the belly of a fish.
> The eyes of ordinary persons should resemble
> a blue lotus...

Tibetan art oscillates between the body that is a temple, creative rhythms of nature and the awakening of the mind: from the form to the absolute of non-form. The scrolls, sculptures and *maṇḍalas* were the iconic representation of transcendental meditation. Icon is the embodied Divine, the unmanifest *(amūrta)* concretised into the manifest icon *(mūrti)* of a two-dimensional painting or a three-dimensional image. The scrolls are called *thaṅka*—'painting on a flat surface'. *'Thaṅ'* means 'a flat plain' with the specifying suffix *'ka'*. The images are known as *sku* or 'bodily form' in the sacred round.

The Tibetan *Vinaya* enjoins that the monastic interiors should be embellished. It relates that Anāthapiṇḍada wanted to decorate the walls of the Jetavana Monastery that he was about to offer to the Buddha. The monks did not know what to do. The Buddha said that all kinds of colours should be employed, and should represent a *Yakṣa* holding a baton at the entrance, the Grand Miracle and the Wheel of Existence in the vestibule, *jātakas* in the cloister and so on. The *Vinaya* continues that when the paintings were completed, men came to admire them bringing about many conversions. Thus paintings and sculptures were 'Visual *Dharma*' constituting transcendental vision in the aesthetics of beauty and the yonder shore of *pāramitās*. Each *tantra* was represented as a *maṇḍala* with the main deity in the central circle, accompanied by others in three concentric squares, with wrathful guardians at the four gates. The *Mahāvairocanābhisambodhi Tantra* has a *maṇḍala* of Abhisambodhi Vairocana surrounded by 121 deities.

Four major denominations of Buddhism arose in Tibet, with numerous sub-sects. The oldest of them was the Nyingmapa that goes back to Padmasambhava who was responsible for the first monastery in Tibet. The denominations were formally designated in AD 1062. The teachings of Atīśa and disciple Ḥbrom-ston (AD 1008-1064) with their centrality of the path of meditation and strict monastic discipline became the Kadampa. They were assimilated into the Gelukpa four centuries later. By the 11th century, the Sakyapa and Kargyupa denominations came into existence. The Sakya was founded by Gyalpo in AD 1073. The Sakya became powerful under the Mongol dynasty of Yüan in China (AD 1260-1324) by becoming their Imperial Preceptors. Tsoṅ-kha-pa (AD 1357-1419) founded the Gelukpa denomination in the early 15th century AD. They absorbed the Kadampa and became most powerful under the Dalai Lamas. Each denomination had primary deities, important monastic centres and spiritual lineages, maintained in precise records and painted on the outer square of the *thaṅka* of a deity or of a guru.

The pre-Buddhist religion of Tibet is Bon which originated in the kingdom of Zhangzhung. Its beliefs and deities were absorbed by Buddhism, while the Bon Canon was modelled after the Buddhist Canon of the Kanjur and Tanjur. The Buddhist pantheon became the inspiration for Bon theogony.

The Nepalese queen of Sroṅ-btsan-sgam-po, Bhṛikuṭī brought the first sculpture of Buddha Śākyamuni in AD 639. It was installed at Jokhang in Lhasa. The second image of Śākyamuni reached Lhasa as a part of the dowry of his Chinese queen Wencheng. The dowry of Queen Bhṛikuṭī, who is worshiped by the Tibetans as Green Tārā, included images of Akṣobhyavajra, Maitreya, and a sandalwood statue of Tārā. This is the earliest reference to an image of Tārā. Clay and stone sculptures, rock carvings, gilt copper statues, ungilded brass statues that have come down from the Imperial period of Tibet (*c.* 600-842) indicate a flourishing tradition. The statue of a queen from the 8th century personifying Sarasvatī shows remarkable similarities with the fashions of the Shahi rulers whose empire included the western Himalayas, Afghanistan and the Western Tarim basin during the 8th and 9th centuries.

The Buddha is a person who has attained Enlightenment that leads to release from the cycle of births and deaths. There is the historical Buddha, namely, Śākyamuni who is a *Samyak-Sambuddha* or Perfectly Enlightened One. He expounds the newly discovered teaching for the welfare of all sentients beings. Besides, there are *pratyeka-Buddhas* who do not expound the teaching though they have attained complete Enlightenment. Besides the historical Buddha, there are five past Buddhas

who preceded him: Vipaśyin, Śikhin, Krakucchanda, Kanakamuni and Kāśyapa. Maitreya is the future Buddha. Thus there are Seven Supreme Buddhas. There are several classifications of the Buddhas, for instance, the three Buddhas of the three times: Dīpaṅkana of the past, Śākyamuni of the present, and Maitreya of the future. The 'Buddha principle' manifests itself in varied forms. There are five main Transcendental Buddhas: Amitābha, Akṣobhya, Vairocana, Ratnasambhava and Amoghasiddhi. They are supra-mundane and can be represented in three ways *(trikāya)*; as monks *(nirmāṇa-kāya),* as donning royal apparel and jewellery *(sambhoga-kāya),* and aniconically *(Dharma-kāya).* Vajradhara heads the hierarchical scheme of Vajrayāna, and a large number of Buddhas emanate from him, all in union with their consorts *(Yab-Yum).* They culminate in the complex iconography of Kālacakra. The Buddha is also a synonym for the Eternal Truth or ultimate reality of Buddha-nature, which is devoid of form, colour, historical dates, psychological nuances or philosophical questions.

Buddhas

Śākyamuni: Buddha of the Present

Away from the illusory scene of transience and impermanence, is the Enlightened One: Śākyamuni, the Sage of the Śākyas. He has overcome the temptations of Māra and his demons in their innumerable aspects, some terrifying, some monstrous and some voluptuous. The intense inner struggle of Gautama makes him an immediately human figure to us. He calls the Earth Goddess as witness, by his earth-touching gesture or *bhūmi-sparśa mudrā.* The right hand stretches down to the earth, the palm inside and all fingers straight. By this gesture, he destroys all the demons of the earth. While the right hand of Śākyamuni is in the earth-touching gesture, his left hand holds the alms bowl. On either side of the lion throne are two leaping lions. Bodhicaryāvatāra says, 'All is to be vanquished by me, none can vanquish me. In this way shall I remain self-confident.' The lion is a symbol of our steadfast pursuit of wholesome striving. To overcome poisonous delusions is the fruit of Enlightenment.

Flanking Śākyamuni are his two chief disciples– Śāriputra and Maudgalyāyana (p. 23). They are the epitomes of ideal disciples whose example others should follow. Usually each of them hold a mendicant's staff and bowl.

Śākyamuni sits on a throne which indicates that he has perfected the six transcendences. These six *pāramitās* are represented by six animals: the *garuḍa* or divine eagle at the top is the first *pāramitā* of charity *(dāna).* The two young *nāga*s stand for moral excellence *(śīla-pāramitā).* The two dolphins or *makaras* are symbols of forbearance *(kṣānti-pāramitā).* The two dwarfs or *vāmana*s represent endurance *(vīrya-pāramitā).* The two elephants stand for meditation *(dhyāna-pāramitā).* The two lions below the lotus are the highest perfection of wisdom *(prajñā-pāramitā).*

Brahmā on the right and Indra on the left are the Lords of Earth and Heaven respectively. They are the totality of space. They request the Buddha to set the Wheel of *Dharma* in motion, for the love of them who are hesitating between truth and falsehood, and wavering between good and evil. It is to Brahmā that the Buddha speaks his first words after Enlightenment. It is Brahmā who first uses the word 'Tathāgata' in addressing the Buddha.

Speaking of the Enlightenment, Śākyamuni himself states that, the attainment of Enlightenment dissolves all phenomena into peace and tranquility, into active fragments of the interior life, the shadows of his *sambodhi,* away from the whirlwind of *saṁsāra.* The void of a scroll is the realisation that perturbing visions are nothing but mere images. Solid mountains, wandering clouds,

FACING PAGE: *Rays of spiritual light emanate from the heart of the Buddha. This Divine Radiance resides in human depths as the intimate essence of Being.*

singing birds are but forms of the relative. Form is Emptiness and Emptiness is Form (*rūpaṁ śūnyatā, śūnyatā eva rūpam)* says the *Prajñā-pāramitā*. Forms transmigrate into Emptiness; they show no attachment to Form. They echo the land of Nowhere. No reflecting images soil the Enlightenment of the Solemn One, endowed with the bliss of tranquility, as he remains steady. The moment the Lord obtained omniscience, splendour illumined the world-realms.

The *thaṅka* (p. 21) is in the famous Karma Gadri style, which was a new approach to hieratic art developed in the 16th century by the Incarnate Lama Namkhatashi, with innovations in the treatment of backgrounds, elegance of composition and distinctive use of colours and shading.

Buddha Śākyamuni is in the *mudrā* of turning the *Dharmacakra* or Wheel of *Dharma* (left):

> Thus, monks, among doctrines unheard before,
> in me sight and knowledge arose, wisdom arose,
> knowledge arose, light arose.

Standing at the bottom are Avalokiteśvara and Maitreya. The former represents great compassion, mercy and love, with a vow to save all beings. Maitreya is the Future Buddha. Enlightenment, compassionate benevolence and timeless future unite one to ultra-terrestrial perfection.

ABOVE: *Śākyamuni in the* mudrā *of turning the Wheel of* Dharma (dharmacakra)*. At the bottom of the* thaṅka *are Avalokiteśvara and Maitreya. The three connote Enlightenment, Compassion and the Timeless Future in their ultra-terrestrial perfection.*

Buddha Śākyamuni appears with an ornate nimbus of *nāgas*, goddesses showering flowers and a *garuḍa* with outstretched wings above them.

On the right, four-faced Brahmā, yellow in body, holds the *cakra,* the mark of the universal dominion of a *cakravartin,* and Indra, King of the Gods, white in complexion, with a vase, descended from his elephant Airāvata on the left, offer their homage to the Buddha. Below them are the two chief disciples Śāriputra and Maudgalyāyana. In the centre is a table with offerings, flanked by a donor couple, the wife on the right and husband on the left. It is a pleasing harmony of colours with the reds and gold dominant.

On page 19 is Saṅs-rgyas ḥod-zer or the Divine Radiance of the Buddha. Rays of spiritual light flow forth from the heart of the Buddha who is mysteriously visible from behind the screen of rays. If the rays emanate from the top of his head, they indicate a Buddha; if they emanate from his forehead, they announce the presence of a Bodhisattva, and if rays emerge from his heart, a human being is near.

Maitreya: Future Buddha

Maitreya, the Future Buddha, sits in the *lalita* posture. He is of golden colour, peaceful and

ABOVE: *Śākyamuni in the* bhūmi-sparśa mudrā *summons the Earth as witness to his Enlightenment, as he emerges from the melee of monstrous beings and satanic temptations of Māra. The Seven Buddhas in the upper part of the* thaṅka *depict the historical continuity of spiritual evolution.*

resplendent. His long hair is drawn up in a knot on his head, while part of them hang down the back. The matted locks are his crown. He holds the twig of a *nāgakesara* flower in the right hand, wears no ornament, but has the figure of a miniature *caitya* in his matted hair. The *caitya* in his crown refers to the *stūpa* on Mount Kukkuṭapāda (modern Kukrihar) near Bodhgaya, where Kāśyapa Buddha is lying. When Maitreya leaves his Tuṣita Heaven, descends on earth and goes to the Mount, it will open by magic, and Kāśyapa will give him the robes of a Buddha. The *uṣṇīṣa* or top-knot over his head, the long-lobed ears, and the monastic robe with the right shoulder bare, indicate that he is represented as a Buddha. In Tibet, he is also represented as a Bodhisattva, in the *bhadrāsana,* with ornaments and crown. He holds a vase-shaped pitcher besides the three-forked stick *(tridaṇḍī).* The vase is a sign of speed with which its action removes the hindrances of defilement and with which the initiate attains awakening. It holds the ambrosia of knowledge, which is sprinkled on the head of the initiate during the initiation ritual so that he is purified and awakened with speed. The skin of the black antelope hangs from his left shoulder and indicates that he is the incarnation of compassion *(maitrī).* The black antelope is a very kind-hearted animal, and thus symbolises compassion which makes the *bodhicitta* grow. Maitreya, out

ABOVE: *One of a set of two* thaṅkas *depicting the '35 Buddhas of Confession.' In this* thaṅka *17 Buddhas emerge from the navel of Śākyamuni, the* maṇipūrakacakra. *In this* cakra *the thought aspect appears in the human mind, destroys sorrows, diseases and bestows eternal happiness. A devotee confesses omissions and promises to keep the vows taken: 'Before all the Buddhas I pray that whatsoever little merit I have collected may be shared by all beings.'*

FACING PAGE: *Śākyamuni says: 'Sprinkle water on the seeds of virtue.' (From the story of Prātihārya)*

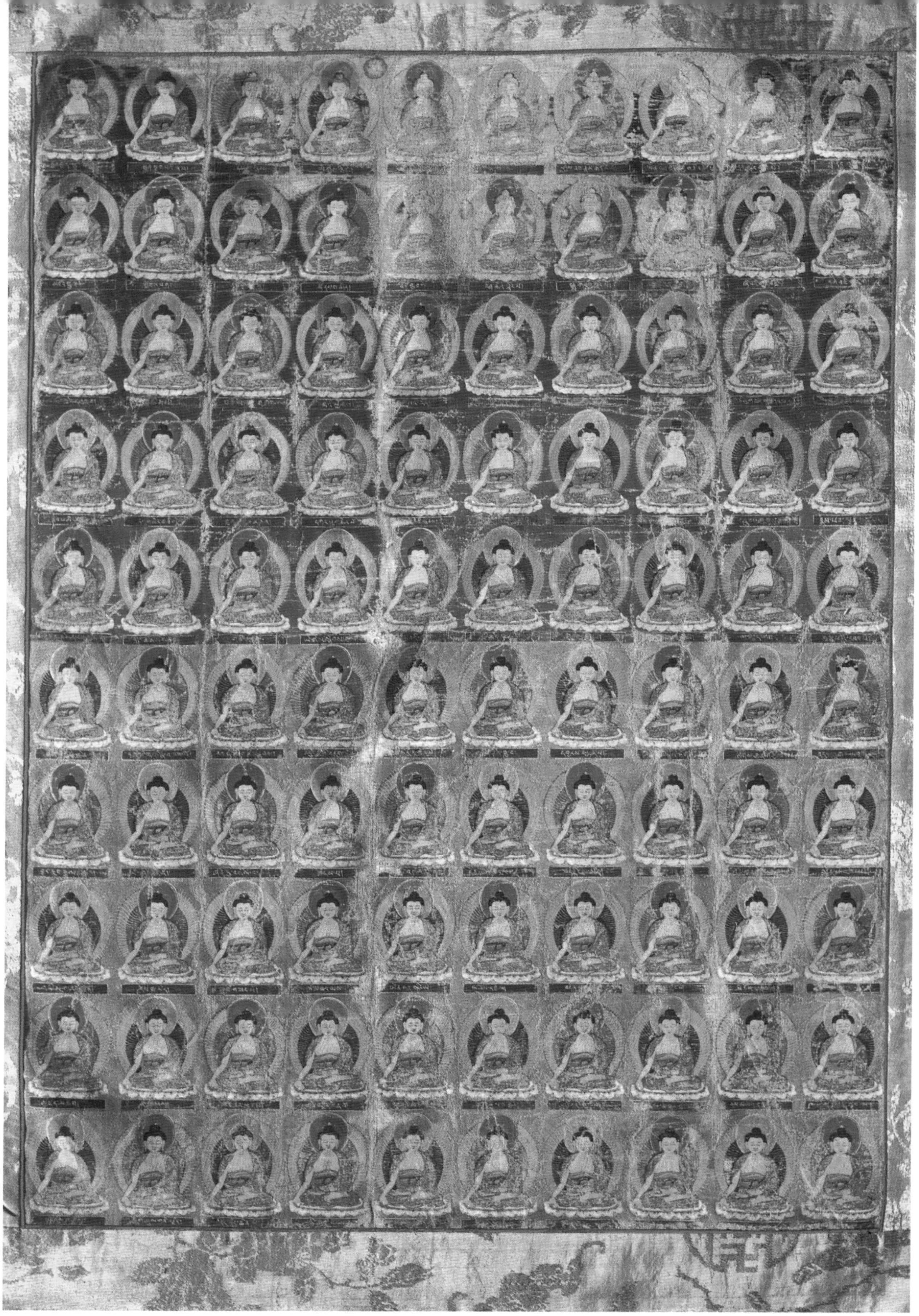

ABOVE: *A 14th-century scroll of the Thousand Buddhas from a Tanggut* stūpa. *Tangguts are the northernmost inhabitants of the Tibeto-Burmese population. The Tanggut State flourished from the 11th to the 13th century. In the 13th century, they were overrun by the Mongol hordes of Ghengis Khan and merged into his empire. This scroll depicts 100 Buddhas of the Thousand Buddhas.*

The Thousand Buddhas

The Thousand Buddhas represent the awareness of the perennial possibilities of the spiritual horizon. Here, the illumined mind is thousand-folded into an ever higher intuition of the infinity of the transcendental. The Thousand Buddhas bless the present aeon of *Bhadrakalpa.* A special scripture, the *Bhadra-kalpika Sūtra* is devoted to them. It was translated into Tibetan in the 8th century. Ever since, the Thousand Buddhas have blessed every Tibetan monastery, where they are found as votive icons over a central image.

In India, a special literary genre was devoted to the thousand names, rather epithets, of a divinity. The thousand names of Viṣṇu are well known as the V*iṣṇu-sahasra-nāma.* Likewise, the Buddha had a thousand epithets which underwent an apotheosis as the Thousand Buddhas, and became a thousand pictures or a thousand icons.

of compassion for all sentient beings, abstained from eating meat from the first moment of the quickening of his *bodhicitta*.

Maitreya is one of the Buddhas of the Three Times (dus-gsum saṅs-rgyas). The other two are Dīpaṅkara and Śākyamuni. He is sitting in his Tuṣita Heaven as a Bodhisattva awaiting the time of descent to the earth. Maitreya is the hope of civilisation expressing the invisible future by means of the visible.

Maitreya with his Disciples Asaṅga and Vasubandhu

The Tibetan artistic tradition represents the Six Jewels and Two Eminents of Buddhist thought. The Six Jewels of Buddhism are Āryadeva and his guru Nāgārjuna, Asaṅga and his younger brother Vasubandhu, Dīṅnāga and Dharmakīrti. Their teachings shine like the sun and they are held in the highest honour for strenuous endeavours to promote the holy teachings. They expounded the *Yogācāra* and *Abhidharma* systems of Buddhist philosophy. Maitreya's rays of Enlightenment inspired Asaṅga and Vasubandhu, the philosopher saints of the 4th century AD. Vasubandhu (p. 28) is shown with a book. Maitreya descends from his heaven and comes in a cloud featured like a rainbow. He holds the *stūpa* in his hands. Asaṅga engaged himself in ceaseless meditational exercises for twelve years on Kukkuṭapāda hill. Here he transported himself by means of *yoga* to heaven where he received Enlightenment from Maitreya and brought down to earth the teachings of Maitreya. Asaṅga was from Gāndhāra. Strongly influenced by Śaivism, he became the founder of a new school of Yogācāra, whose principles he laid down in his main work *Yogācāra-bhūmi-śāstra*. His teachings received wide acceptance in consequence of the belief that he had been miraculously transported to the Tuṣita Heaven, where Maitreya taught him.

Asaṅga's younger brother Vasubandhu gained extraordinary proficiency in the Vedas while very young. He made his mark in Sarvāstivāda, and made a special study of *Abhidharma* philosophy under Saṅghabhadra in Kashmir. Thence he went to Magadha and wrote the *Abhidharma-kośa*, which has since remained a classic. His works on the *Vijñaptimātratā*, logic, and critiques of *Prajñā-pāramitā* are fundamental. He distinguished himself as an abbot of Nalanda. Later he lived and died in Ayodhyā. He combined originality of mind with astounding erudition. He pointed out that the entire universe is nothing but the mind *(citta)*. He was pre-eminently a scholar and preferred the academic attitude to realise the truth.

While the Maitreya school was mainly busy with metaphysical and transcendental speculations, the

FACING PAGE: *The central portion of a* thaṅka *of the Thousand Buddhas of the present aeon of the Bhadrakalpa. Along with the colossal images, such as the two at Bamiyan, they represent the golden radiance of the plurality of the human mind. Immensity and multiplicity are the ineffable truth of life summed up in: 'The unbounded ocean am I.'*

ABOVE: *Maitreya, the Bodhisattva expounds* yogācāra *to Asaṅga and Vasubandhu. Maitreya holds a* stūpa *in his hands as he is about to descend on earth to replenish the five divine wisdoms, represented by the five colours of the rainbow. Asaṅga's white expresses his illumined consciousness. Vasubandhu represents the academic attitude to realise the Truth and as such he holds a book. Asaṅga meditated for twelve years on Kukkuṭapāda Hill, transported himself by* yoga *to the Tuṣita Heaven of Maitreya, and brought down the teachings of the* tantra.

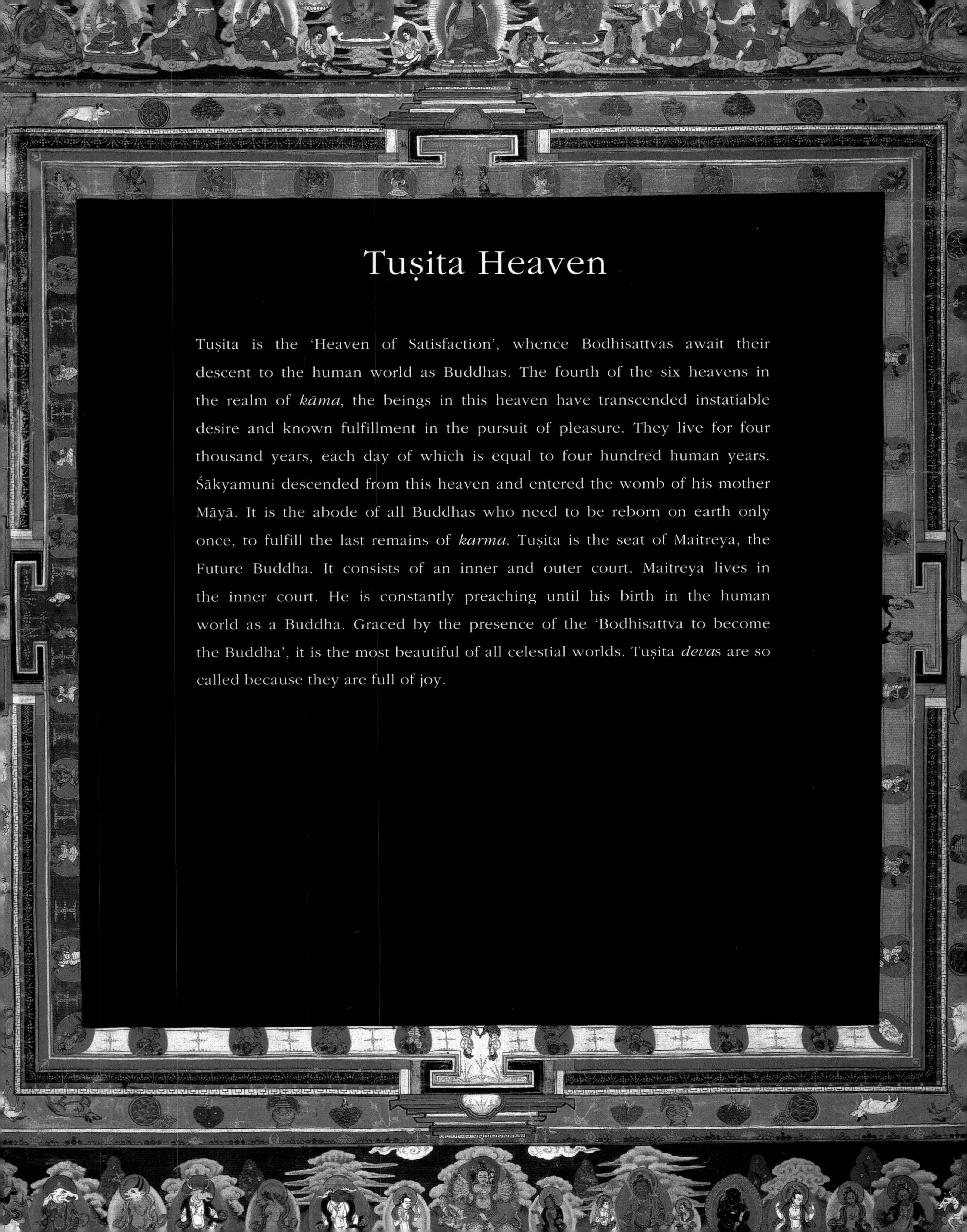

Tuṣita Heaven

Tuṣita is the 'Heaven of Satisfaction', whence Bodhisattvas await their descent to the human world as Buddhas. The fourth of the six heavens in the realm of *kāma*, the beings in this heaven have transcended instatiable desire and known fulfillment in the pursuit of pleasure. They live for four thousand years, each day of which is equal to four hundred human years. Śākyamuni descended from this heaven and entered the womb of his mother Māyā. It is the abode of all Buddhas who need to be reborn on earth only once, to fulfill the last remains of *karma*. Tuṣita is the seat of Maitreya, the Future Buddha. It consists of an inner and outer court. Maitreya lives in the inner court. He is constantly preaching until his birth in the human world as a Buddha. Graced by the presence of the 'Bodhisattva to become the Buddha', it is the most beautiful of all celestial worlds. Tuṣita *deva*s are so called because they are full of joy.

Yogācāra school taught that with the help of mystic charms, spells and invocations, accompanied by music and *mudrās*, so that the state of *samādhi* occurs where thinking as well as non-thinking stop and six-fold physical and mental happiness and *siddhi* is attained.

The *thaṅka* on page 31 is a fine specimen of appliqué scrolls done by stitching together pieces of cloth of various colours. This Maitreya originates from a monastery in the Gobi Desert. He is standing, about to descend to earth to establish the lost truths. The right hand is in the *abhaya mudrā* of conferring fearlessness while the left holds a *campaka* or *nāgakesara* flower over which is a book in *pothi* format topped by the *cakra*.

At the bottom are the offerings of the five senses (Tibetan: ḥdod-yon lṅa) represented by specific symbols. The mirror stands for sight, the silk flowing out of the bowl for touch, the holy cakes for taste, the lute for hearing, and the conch full of curds for scent. With these offerings the devotee sheds his trammels of the *saṁsaric* plane.

Five Transcendental Buddhas

Amitābha

The historic tradition of Śākyamuni evolved into the doctrine of Future Buddhas. They could be in thousands, and we have seen that the Thousand Buddhas were represented frequently in Tibetan scrolls and in miniature votive statuettes hung above a main image, like that of Mahākāla. Besides, new Transcendental Buddhas developed in the Tantric traditions, for instance, Vairocana. They are placed in the centre and four directions: Vairocana in the centre, Amitābha in the west, Akṣobhya in the east, Ratnasambhava in the south and Amoghasiddhi in the north. Also, existing deities were substituted by new ones, for example, Amitābha became a substitute for Śākyamuni, Avalokiteśvara for Brahmā and Mahāsthāmaprāpta for Indra.

Amitābha is Infinite Light. He is the synthesis of the purity of the *māyā*-body with its appropriate signs in the clarity of mind *(citta)*, in its essential nature the same as light (don-gyi ḥod-gsal). He is the inexpressible luminous essence, represented in his western paradise of Sukhāvatī, and sometimes by himself as a Tathāgata. Red in colour, he is in monastic robes with the vase for alms placed in his hands in the *samādhi-mudrā* of contemplation. He is the *nirmāṇa-kāya,* the preparation for the spiritual maturity of his devotees. He has to be distinguished from his *sambhoga-kāya* form, Amitāyus (Infinite Life), ruling over Sukhāvatī, resplendent with diadem and royal ornaments. The third form in Lamaist dogmatics is the *Dharma-kāya* called *Ananta-prabha* (Infinite Splendour).

FACING PAGE: *An appliqué* thaṅka *of Maitreya created by stitching together pieces of cloth and silk of various colours. Maitreya is standing ready to descend to earth to establish lost truths. The superposition of the book and* cakra *on a* campaka *flower denotes the turning of the* dharma-cakra*. At the bottom are the offerings of the five senses represented by symbols. the mirror stands for sight, flowing silk for touch, holy cakes for taste, lute for hearing, and the conch full of curd for scent. Through these offerings the devotee sheds his* samsar*ic bonds.*

Trayastriṁśa

Trayastriṁśa is the 'Heaven of Thirty-three Gods' in the realm of Kāmadhātu. It is located on a plateau on top of Mount Sumeru where thirty-three gods, including their king Śakra (or India) live. Śakra lives in his palace Sudarsāna in the centre, and the other gods live on four peaks in the four directions, eight gods to a peak. They have a long life span of a hundred divine years, each day of which is equal to a hundred human years. Trayastriṁśa is one of the six *deva*-worlds. It is surrounded by five ramparts, guarded by *nāga*s, *suparṇa*s, *kumbhāṇḍa*s, *yakṣa*s and *caturmahārājika* gods. The Buddha went to this heaven to preach *abhidharma* to his mother. He spent three months preaching, seated on the throne of Śakra, in the seventh year after his Enlightenment. Maudgalyāyana, one of the two chief disciples of the Buddha, paid several visits to this paradise to learn the stories of those dwelling there, so that he may recount them for the edification of humans on earth. Śakra deposited in the Cūḍāmaṇi Stūpa the hair of Prince Siddhārtha, cut off by the latter when he renounced the world. Goddesses from Trayastriṁśa come down to bathe in the Anavatapta Lake (modern: Mansarovar). The nymphs of Trayastriṁśa are famous in literature for their beauty, and the gods are most handsome.

On the right Amitābha (p. 35) is flanked by Padmapāṇi Avalokiteśvara and on the left by Vajrapāṇi Mahāsthāmaprāpta. Padmapāṇi holds a lotus blossom and Mahāsthāmaprāpta has a *vajra* on a lotus held aloft in the hands. His mount is the peacock, sometimes represented on the right and the left of the pedestal of his throne. The peacock throne of Iran is reminiscent of the ancient Amitābha cult.

Intellectual discrimination and sense perceptions are converted into transcendental faculties of inner vision and spiritual discernment in the practice of meditation: this is the specific function of Amitābha. He is one with the Wisdom of Discriminating Clear Vision *(pratyavekṣanā-jñāna)*. Pure, uncreated, he is self-luminous and all-pervading. His symbolic syllable is *HRIḤ: H* is the sound of breath, the symbol of all life; *R* is the sound

ABOVE: *Amitābha in his Western Paradise of Sukhāvatī. Pious and devoted beings lead a blissful life in this Pure Land by reciting his name. In a deeper sense it represents a state of mind flooded by the radiance that emanates from Amitābha, the Transcendental* (amita) *Light* (ābha).

of fire; *I* is the intensity of vibration which stands for the highest spiritual activity. Conceptualisation proliferates, sparking new ideas, and lording over it is Amitābha. His red colour bears the meaning that compassion is enamoured of all living beings. The colour of Enamour *(rāga)* is red in the Buddhist tradition. According to the principles of *yoga*, the human personality is adduced into Amitābha's world by a projection of the conscious principle.

In some *thaṅkas* the central figure of Amitābha is surrounded by representations of the Five Tathāgatas. The first figure on the top is that of Amoghasiddhi (green) followed by those of Vairocana (white), Akṣobhya (blue), Ratnasambhava (yellow), Amitābha (red). The Five Tathāgatas are repeated ten times, making up a total of 50 inclusive of the central figure.

Amitābha as a *sambhoga-kāya* has an elaborate crown and resplendent jewels which distinguish him as a *sambhoga-kāya* in all regal splendour. He wears the six ornaments: earrings, necklace, body-garland, armlets, wristbands and anklets. He can be identified by his red complexion, and his hands in the *samādhi-mudrā* of meditation. At the bottom of the lotus on the left and right are two peacocks, characteristic mounts of the Tathāgata. Two Bodhisattvas, Padmapāṇi and Vajrapāṇi, stand gracefully on either side of the green throne. The remaining six of the eight Bodhisattvas are seated, three on each side. All the eight Bodhisattvas are of golden reddish colour. The names of the eight Bodhisattvas are: Padmapāṇi Avalokiteśvara, Vajrapāṇi Mahāsthāmaprāpta, Samantabhadra, Mañjuśrī, Kṣitigarbha, Ākāśagarbha, Nīvaraṇa-viṣkambhin and Maitreya.

Amitābha is absorbed in the knowledge of marvellous discernment. He presides over the virtues of the attestation of *bodhi*. He symbolizes the explanation of *Dharma* and of the removal of doubts by Vairocana. Examining the degree of the development of beings, he makes known that all *Dharmas* are originally pure by their intrinsic nature. He is also called Lokeśvara-Rāja—King of Kings of the People *(loka)*.

Amitābha belongs to the lotus family: Vairocana enters the Tathāgata's pure lotus *samādhi* that is the fundamental nature of all *Dharmas*, and then radiates a light the colour of a crimson lotus which illuminates the immeasurable western world.

Amitābha is depicted with the eight Bodhisattvas flanking his lotus-seat, four on each side. The splendours of Sukhāvatī, 'prosperous, rich, good to live in, fertile, lovely' are represented in this depiction adorned by a tree. Below Amitābha is a lotus miraculously sprung up from the conscious principle of a human personality transported to Amitābha's heaven. Out of the god's heart a hook of light is projected, which draws towards itself the

FACING PAGE: *One of the earliest Tibetan* thaṅkas *available, this depiction of Amitābha is a shining example of the exquisite art of the 11th /12th century in the Pāla style. The elaborate crown and resplendent jewels present Amitābha in the* sambhoga-kāya *or Enjoyment Body in regal splendour. The five Goddesses of Protection* (Pañcarakṣās) *are represented at the bottom.*

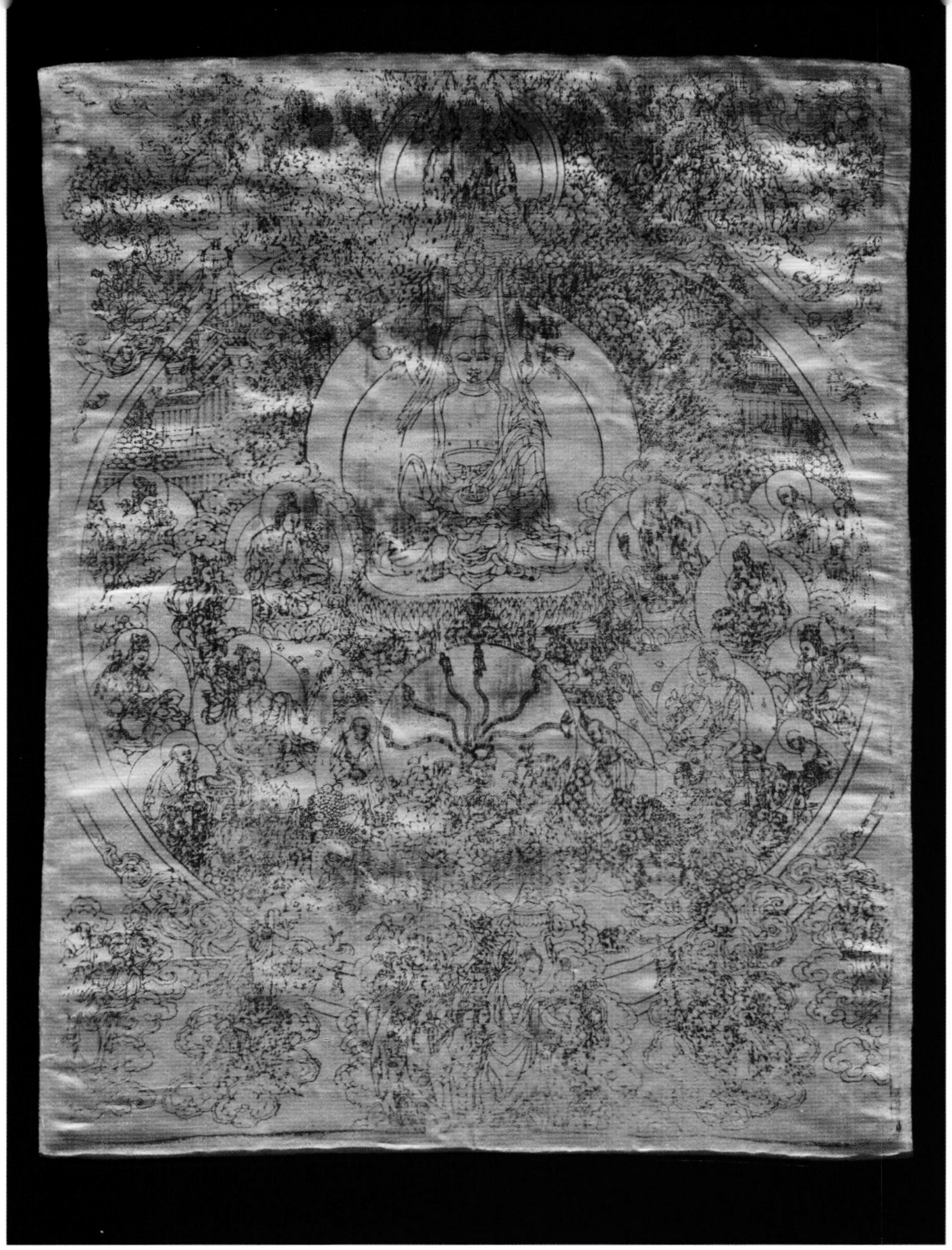

devotee's conscious principle, represented by a luminous globe, the size of a grain, residing in his heart. This principle, thus attracted, disappears and is dissolved into the god's heart, with which it is substantially unified; next, it once again emanates from it, in order to give birth to the new divine incarnation in the centre of the lotus, miraculously sprung up in front of the god.

Amitāyus

The following attributes distinguish Amitāyus from Amitābha: Amitābha is in the *dhyāna-mudrā,* with an alms-bowl; a *nirmāṇa-kāya,* he wears monastic robes: Amitāyus is in the *dhyāna-mudrā,* with an *amṛta-kalaśa*—an ambrosia-filled vase—with leaves of the aśoka tree, symbolizing a long life without care. A *sambhoga-kāya* he wears royal ornaments.

ABOVE: *Amitābha or the Buddha of Transcendental Light, in his Pure Land of Perfect Bliss. Among his 48 vows, he had pledged to bring all sentient beings, who placed their hopes of salvation in him, to his Pure Land. Those who had committed the five cardinal sins would not be allowed in here. Devotees adopted a new and simple path of reciting the name of Amitābha to gain rebirth in the Pure Land.*

The conceptualisation of Enlightenment as a flash of illumination led to the apotheosis of Infinite Light as Amitābha. An important function of deities is healing and long life. This healing aspect was apotheosized as Amitāyus. Amitāyus was invoked to cure a person suffering from ill-health, but after death he went to the world of Amitābha. Amitāyus bestows long life and, usually holds the vase of ambrosia in his hands which are in the *dhyāna-mudrā* or gesture of meditation. He wears a diadem and is richly adorned with royal ornaments. His body colour is deep red and his blue hair flows over either side of the shoulders.

Painted scrolls and icons of Amitāyus are found in abundance in Tibet, Mongolia and also in Transbaikalian Buryatia because of the firm faith

ABOVE: *Sublime and luminous in the transparency of the fading colours and delicate lines of this* thaṅka *sits the White Amitāyus. The* thaṅka *represents the bliss of the spiritual vision of its inimitable painter. The diaphanous charm of the colours radiates serenity, raising the spirit into the realm of Life Immense. White Amitāyus is surrounded by 54 manifestations; the addition of a second* thaṅka *takes the number of manifestations to the auspicious 108 emanations.*

of the people in his powers of prolonging life. For everlasting life (Tibetan: tshe-sgrub) a sacrament to Amitāyus is celebrated on an auspicious day. Crowds throng to the temple to receive blessings. Every village performs it at least once a year for the long life of the community.

Maṇḍala of Amitāyus

The central deity of the *maṇḍala* is Amitāyus/Tshe-dpag-med, embraced by his consort, Pāṇḍaravāsinī, 'The White-Robed One'. Both of them are red in colour. Amitāyus, the Lord of Boundless Life, is the active aspect of Amitābha, the embodiment of Wisdom of Inner Vision. Amitāyus appears as a Prince of *Dharma,* and as such his virtues are symbolised by the insignia of royalty like the crown and other adornments—he is a *sambhoga-kāya.* He represents the active side of his nature as the Giver of Infinite Life, no longer caught in the narrow confines of the ego. The infinite life of Amitābha becomes the source of life that is boundless. Amitāyus is seated, and his hands lie in his lap in the *samādhi-mūdra* of meditation. They hold the tshe-bum—vase of ambrosia.

The consort of Amitāyus, Paṇḍaravāsinī, is the embodiment of fire, full of attachment *(rāga-raktā).* As such she is red and is conspicuous by her flowing white scarf. The lotus below the *Yab-Yum* is the symbol of his lotus family.

Amitāyus is placed on the abstract plane of the *maṇḍala,* in the elemental cosmogram of the world. His identity is contrasted to that of Amitābha, and it is in later Vajrayāna schools that he attains his individual popularity, to provide immortality through liturgy. Those initiated into his mysteries were rescued from death. Tshepame, the God of Infinite Life, became *chime*—'immortality'.

ABOVE: *Amitāyus, the Lord of Boundless Life is a* sambhoga-kāya *adorned with royal ornaments.*

FACING PAGE: *Anantaprabha in the* Dharma-kāya *manifestation of Amitāyus in the Nyingmapa denomination. He is the absolute, the symbol of transcendental reality. The five sins that make the texture of* saṁsāra, *constitute the transcendental consciousness, and are transfigured into luminous forms. The luminosities, reflected in the richness of colours of this* thaṅka *are the 'light-voidness' of spiritual potentiality.*

Like the central figure, all are *Yab-Yum* or in union, as is clear from the circlets enclosing another smaller circlet. The figures are luminosities scintillating in colours of deeper meaning: 'Enormous clusters of light rays pouring forth.'

The psychosphere of the *maṇḍala* is constituted by the three external rims of fire, the *vajra* or thunderbolt, and the lotus. The outermost rim of fire burns the sins of the meditator, while that of the *vajra* solidifies the adamantine plane of the practitioner so that he can become a *vajrasattva* or *vajra*-being to undertake the rites and is enabled for contemplation. The inner rim of lotuses finally purifies the heart of the devotee as he approaches the portals of the *sanctum sanctorum* which can be seen in the four directions with fluttering banners.

The nine-deity *samaya-maṇḍala* comprises the central deity with eight manifestations in the four cardinal directions and in the four intermediate corners (p.41). In most *maṇḍalas* nine forms the central core, with numerous possibilities of addition in concentric circles and portals of the *maṇḍala* palace. The eight directions have to be sanctified for the hallowing of the immanence of the divine. The *maṇḍala* can be in a symbolic form, one of the three ways a *maṇḍala* can be delineated. The *Mahāvairocana Sūtra* says there are three ways of expression: *akṣara* (Sanskrit letters), *mudrā* (signs) and *bimba* (images). In *akṣara,* the deities are

ABOVE: *Amitāyus with a hundred emanations symbolises the Tibetan blessings: 'May you live a hundred autumns.'*

FACING PAGE: *The nine emanations of Amitāyus prolong life. They are: Amitāyus in the centre, surrounded by Vajra, Ratna, Padma, Karma, Guṇa, Jñāna, Acala, and Samantadarśī. They grant life eternal.*

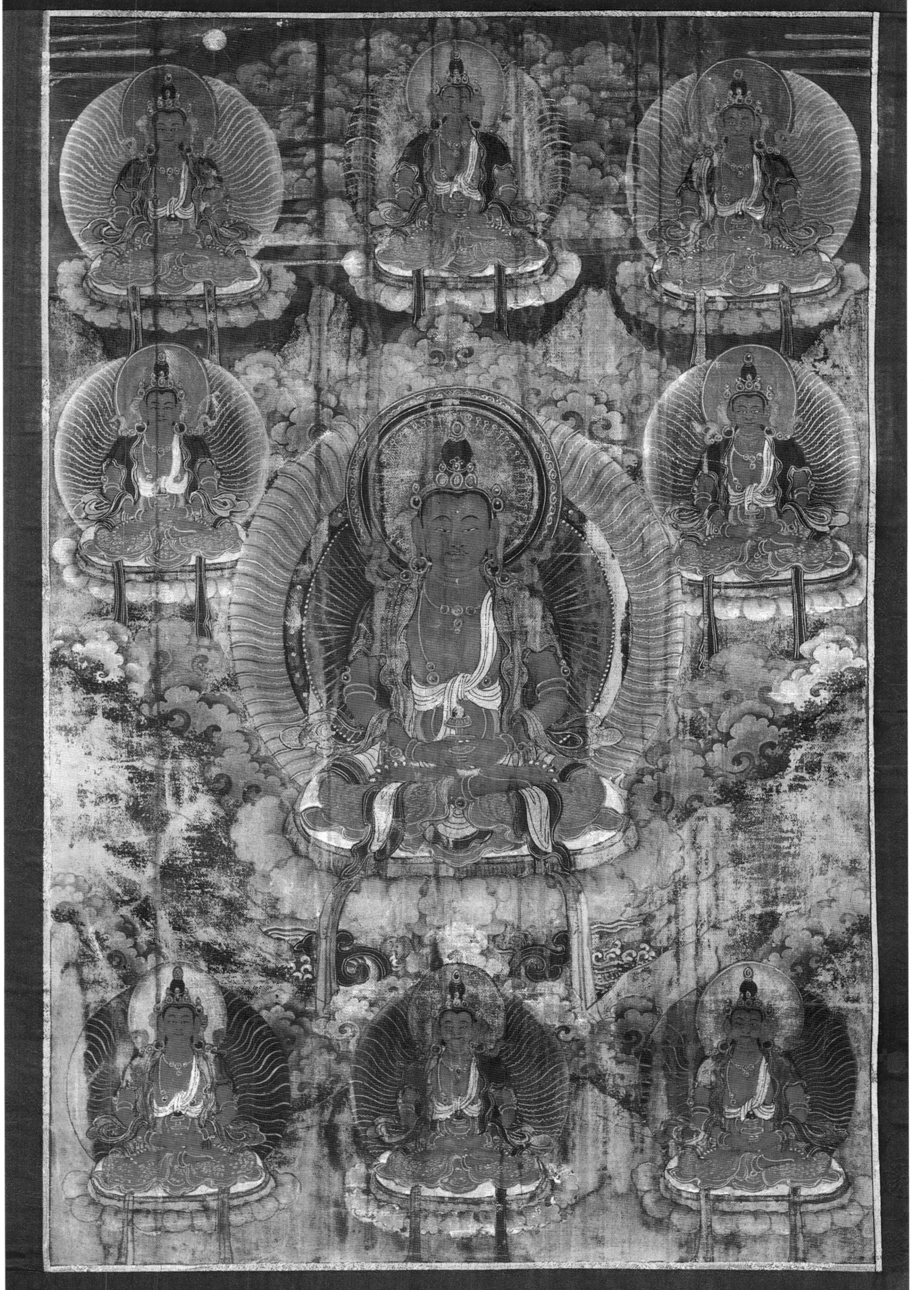

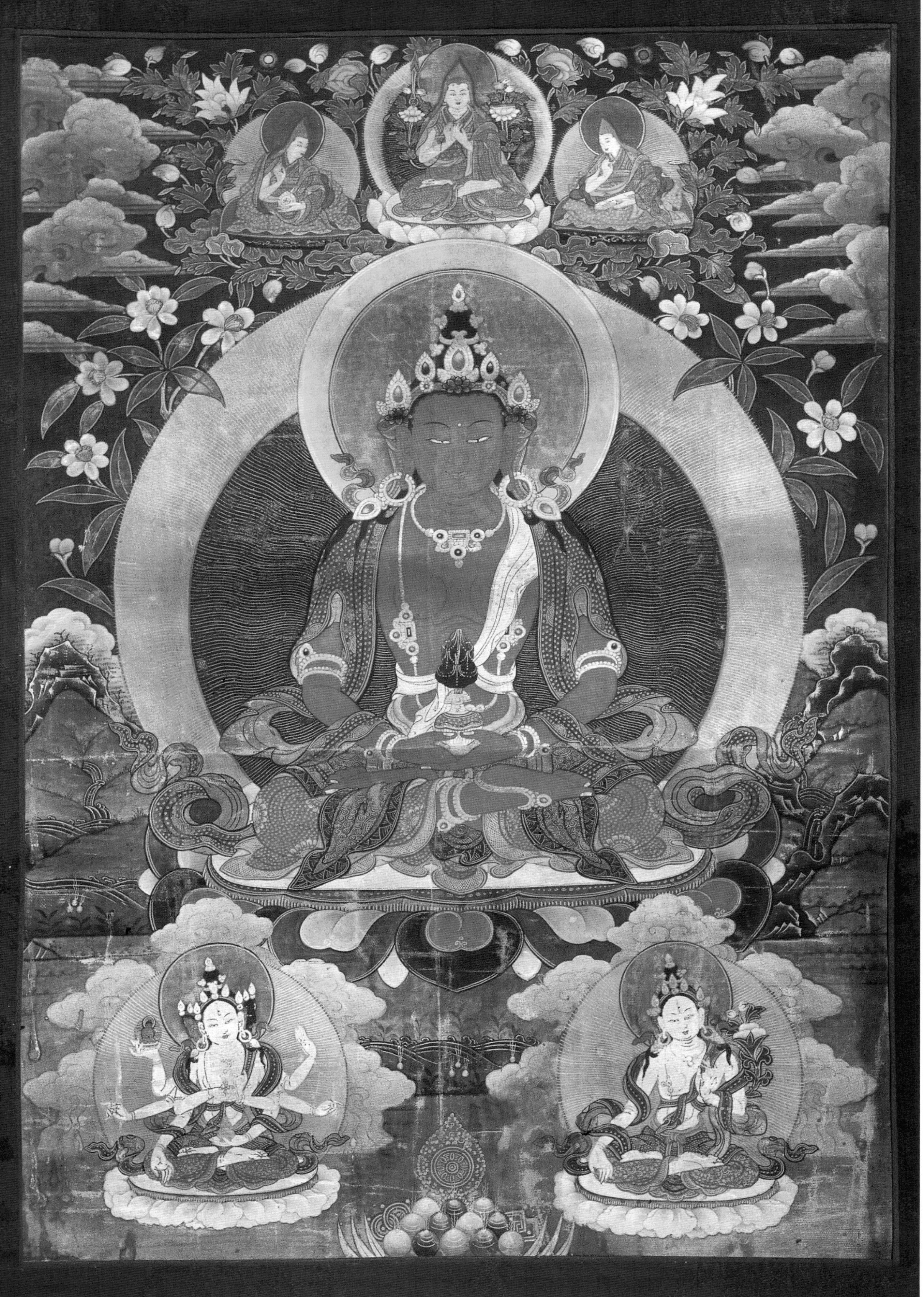

represented by *bījas* or syllables, in *mudrā* by symbols *(samaya),* and in *bimba* by the physical forms with the characteristic marks, anthropomorphically.

The *maṇḍala* of Amitāyus was integral to longevity rites (tshe chog). In these rites, a *maṇḍala* or golden or gilded statue, a scripture, and a golden or gilded *stūpa,* all these three pertaining to Amitāyus, are placed on the altar as the three mysteries of the body, speech and mind of Amitāyus. He is enthroned in his *maṇḍala* surrounded by his eight aspects, to symbolise his omnipresence and to invoke his omnipotence for the officiant. The Lama dispenses blessings as *amṛta* or drops of consecrated water, as white

ABOVE: A thaṅka *of the Thousand Amitāyus. It has 333 Amitāyus and one in the centre. Thousand represents the omnipotence of the grace of the invoked deity. It was a well-established practice in Tibet to paint scrolls to propitiate a Thousand Amitāyus to prolong life.*

FACING PAGE: *Amitāyus with Uṣṇīṣavijayā (left) and White Tārā (right).*

pills of longevity (tsheril) made of flour and sugar, and as amulet thread. The officiant envisions his body filled with purity and whiteness, as if a pure moon is reflected in his heart. This becomes the psychosomatic point of re-integration of the body.

In the scroll on the left, the nine forms of Amitāyus are depicted: Vajra-Amitāyus, Ratna-Amitāyus, Padma-A$^{\underline{o}}$, Karma-A$^{\underline{o}}$, Guṇa-A$^{\underline{o}}$, Jñāna-A$^{\underline{o}}$, Acala-A$^{\underline{o}}$, Samantadarśī-A$^{\underline{o}}$, and Amitāyus proper in the middle. For everlasting life, a sacrament to Amitāyus is celebrated on an auspicious day.

One Hundred and Eight Amitāyus

108 is an auspicious number, showering blessings of a long and happy life on the patron who gets the scroll painted. The placement of the 108 Amitāyus is rendered by a sensitive artist in a manner that enhances the aesthetic appeal of a well-known theme: Amitāyus is in the centre, and on the top is Tsoṅ-kha-pa flanked by his two disciples. At the bottom are White Tārā of Seven Eyes on the left, and Uṣṇīṣavijayā on the left.

The nine-deity *maṇḍala* of Amitāyus has his nine manifestations of the mystic families of Vajra, Ratna, Padma, Karma, Guṇa, Jñāna, Acala and Samantadarśin. On the top are teachers and deities.

Sublime and luminous in the transparency of its fading colours and preserving the majesty of

ABOVE: *A nine-deity maṇḍala of Amitāyus with his manifestations in the nine mystic families of Vajra, Ratna, Padma, Karma, Guṇa, Jñāna, Acala, and Samantadarśī.*

FACING PAGE: *Red Amitāyus in the centre with his eight other manifestations on the petals of the lotus ensures a full span of life. The four* lokapālas *or guardians of the directions are represented in the four corners.*

ABOVE: *The nine emanations of Amitāyus endow life with nine categories of consciousness* (vijñāna).

FACING PAGE: *The 108 representations of Amitāyus for an auspicious flow of a long life of a hundred years, is depicted by the vessel of ambrosia* (amṛta). *The branch of the aśoka tree represents a hale and hearty life, without any sorrow* (a-śoka).

its delicate lines the bliss of the spiritual vision of its inimitable painter, sits White Amitāyus in the hallowed posture of the lotus. The diaphanous charm of the colours radiates serenity, raising the spirit into the realm of Life Immense. White Amitāyus belongs to the tradition of Mitrayogin's teachings. The central Amitāyus is surrounded by his 54 manifestations, so this scroll had a second one to make up the auspicious number of 108. Paintings of White Amitāyus are rare.

Akṣobhya

The tradition of Akṣobhya developed along with that of Amitābha. Monk Laugākṣin who translated *Sukhāvatī-vyūha,* the basic scripture of Amitābha into Chinese in the 2nd century AD, was also responsible for the translation of *Akṣobhya-vyūha.* Five centuries later (AD 706-713) monk Bodhiruci followed the same practice and translated both these scriptures. While the paradise of Amitābha was in the west, that of Akṣobhya was in the east; the east and west were complimentary. These two parallel streams open up new perspectives in the study of the genesis of Vajrayāna Buddhism. The lead role played by women in Abhirati, the paradise of Akṣobhya, distinguishes it from other paradises. In later Buddhist tradition, Akṣobhya, follows Amitābha among the Five Tathāgatas.

Akṣobhya emanates from the blue syllable *HŪṀ.* His blue colour is to subjugate demons. His chest emits a blue light which illumines the innumerable worlds of the east. His mount is a blue elephant. He has one face and two arms. He touches the earth with his right hand in the *bhūmisparśa-mudrā,* sits in the adamantine posture *(vajra-paryaṅka),* and his left hand rests on the lap. He is primordial consciousness. He is a transpersonalised substitute of the historic Śākyamuni. In *Akṣobhya-vyūha,* Śākyamuni recounts to Śāriputra on the Vulture Peak how Akṣobhya made a vow, and expounds to him the merits and the splendour of his paradise.

Akṣobhya, the 'unshakeable' symbolises a firm *bodhicitta* or resolve to Enlightenment, a firmness equal to that of the *vajra.* Absorbed in the perfection of mirror-contemplation *(ādarśa-jñāna)* he destroys demons and passions and presides over the deities who symbolise the pure *bodhicitta.* Dwelling in the adamantine and majestically adorned world in the east, he embodies the virtues of *bodhicitta.*

Akṣobhya, Mi-ḥkhrugs-pa or Mi-bskyod-pa in Tibetan, is usually represented with the Five Buddhas. Paintings showing him individually are uncommon. In the *Advaya-vajra-saṅgraha* he is described as originating 'from the blue syllable *HŪṀ* which is placed on the orb of the sun'. He

FACING PAGE: *Akṣobhya of the Eastern Paradise of Abhirati is the counterpart of Amitābha of the Western Paradise. The Abhirati Paradise is distinguished from others by the leading role played in it by women. The gynocentric emphasis is the centrality of the feminist ideal formulated in the* Prajñā-pāramitās.

is two-armed and one-faced, exhibits the earth-touching *mudrā* and sits in the adamantine pose. He represents the primordial cosmic element of *vijñāna* or consciousness. He is the embodiment of the *vajra* family and represents the winter season, noon-time, pungent taste, faculty of hearing, the element of ether and sound, and the *ca* (palatal) group of letters.

The name Akṣobhya—the Immoveable, the Unshakeable—connotes the Absolute Being or Primordial Consciousness. 'Akṣobhya originated as a symbol of the unchangeableness of the Buddha's condition. When Supreme Enlightenment has been achieved, he who has partaken of it can never lose possession of it: Enlightenment has transferred him to a spiritual plane which is the kingdom of the Absolute, symbolically referred to as "the Diamond Sphere".'

Vairocana

Four-faced Vairocana symbolises germinal luminosity. Everything emanates from him. By raising oneself to superior spiritual levels alone can one be initiated into Vairocana. As the great scholar, Abhayākaragupta says in his book on tantric ritual, *Vajrāvalī:*

> Just as the milk of a lioness
> Is not to be put in a vessel of earth,
> So also the *Supreme Yoga Tantra* is
> Not to be given to unworthy vessels.

Vairocana has four faces, is seated in the diamond posture, is white, effulgent like the sun, and wears a bejewelled crown. His ideal essence is present in the four directions of space: hence the four faces. He wears the five ornaments: a crown to indicate mirror-like knowledge; earrings indicating discriminative knowledge; a necklace symbolising equality of knowledge; bracelets on arms and feet signifying *Dharmadhātu* knowledge, and a sacred belt indicative of procedure-of-duty knowledge. His hands are in the *Dharmacakra-mudrā.* Vairocana in the centre means *Dharmatā-jñāna* or pure knowledge as the central substratum of being.

The painting of Vairocana is the essence of *Yoga Tantras* which consists of meditation. It is the sustenance, the *ādhāra,* of symbolic expression. The conventional visual image is the direct vehicle of realisation. The many divinities represent different moments of the meditational process. In meditation the various categories of phenomenal appearance are re-absorbed into the indiscriminate whole that transcends all conditions.

Durgati-pariśodhana Vairocana

The *maṇḍala* of *Durgati-pariśodhana* is meant to ward off sufferings, release one from the path of

FACING PAGE: *Vairocana, the Transcendental Sun, symbolises universal light that transcends all limitations. He is the radiance of cosmic knowledge. He is pure white, and suppresses obtuseness and ignorance. He resides atop Mount Sumeru in Akaniṣṭha Heaven, the most subtle of the transcendental realms of meditation* (dhyāna-bhūmi).

evil rebirth, and obtain unsurpassable and perfect Enlightenment. One who meditates everyday at dawn and acts in conformity with its *tantra*, and makes effort to produce the highest divine *yoga* with its three stages of concentration, succeeds in eliminating evil destinies.

In the centre of the *maṇḍala* sits Śākyasiṁha, golden in colour, with his hands in the *Dharmacakra mudrā,* and wearing ornaments, that is, he is a *sambhoga-kāya*. He is inside a white *stūpa*, and accompanied by eight goddesses. The *Niṣpanna-yogāvalī* manual on *maṇḍalas* by Abhayākaragupta who lived in the 12th century, describes Śākyasiṁha of the *maṇḍala* of *Durgati-pariśodhana* or the Remover of Misfortunes, as Mahāvairocana of golden complexion in the *Dharmacakra-mudrā,* which destroys *saṁsāra.*

The *Sarva-durgati-pariśodhana Tantra* was translated into Tibetan at the end of the 8th century by the Indian scholar, Śāntigarbha and the Tibetan translator Jayarakṣita. Śāntigarbha took part in the consecration ceremony of Samye, the first Buddhist monastery to be built in Tibet. *Sarva-durgati-pariśodhana* or elimination of all evil destinies is a stage of concentration that releases all beings from the succession of three evil destinies, from phenomenal existence *(saṁsāra)* to Enlightenment. The esoteric significance of the *mudrā* of turning the Wheel of *Dharma* is based on the symbolism

ABOVE: *Durgati-pariśodhana Vairocana frees beings imprisoned by the three evil destinies of* saṁsāra. *He sits in the centre of the lotus, surrounded by eight* uṣṇīṣa *deities, like Jayoṣṇīṣa or 'Supreme Victory' over evil forces, and Uṣṇīṣa-vikiraṇa or 'Supreme Radiation' of the noble values.*

of the wheel. The wheel is associated with the sun and Vairocana is the Great Sun. He dissipates lies and errors, vile and evil, the malevolent and the malicious, just as the sun dispels darkness.

Ratnasambhava

Ratnasambhava (Tibetan: Rin-chen-ḥbyuṅ-gnas or Rin-chen-ḥbyuṅ-ldan) is the fourth of the Five Tathāgatas, yellow in colour, with his right hand in the *varada-mudrā* of bestowing boons, and holding the *cintāmaṇi* jewel. His left hand with an open palm lies on the lap. He is surrounded by a group of eight Bodhisattvas. His individual images and paintings are rare. He represents *samatā-jñāna*—the knowledge of the fundamental identity of things in that all are fleeting images emanated from the depth.

Amoghasiddhi

Amoghasiddhi is the fifth of the Five Tathāgatas located in the north. His colour is green, and he wears monastic robes. He is absolute knowledge that is most effective *(amogha)* in the realization *(siddhi)* of the aims of all beings. He symbolises knowledge through which power spreads. He rides on a *garuḍa* of golden plumage, represents the cosmic element of *saṁskāra* (conformation), and corresponds to the perfection of work.

ABOVE: *Ratnasambhava with 333 emanations. He is the third of the Five Transcedental Buddhas in the* maṇḍala *of Vajradhātu-Vairocana. He represents the knowledge of the fundamental identity of things in that all are fleeting images. Located in the south of the* maṇḍala, *he is yellow and a symbol of creative potential.*

ABOVE: *The 108 manifestations of Ratnasambhava, the fourth of the Five Transcendental Buddhas of the Vajradhátu system. He represents* samatā-jñāna, *the knowledge of the fundamental identity of things.*

FACING PAGE: *Ratnasambhava with his 200 manifestations, sits on a throne of six* pāramitās *where* garuḍa *represents charity* (dāna), *elephant is meditation* (dhyāna), makara *or dolphin is forbearance* (kṣānti) *and the dwarf on the* makara *signifies endurance* (vīrya). *The five Transcendental Buddhas, each with 200 manifestations, constitute the Thousand Buddhas.*

Bodhisattvas

Bodhisattva in Mahāyāna means 'one who has attained enlightenment, can attain *nirvāṇa* or final liberation, but refrains from doing so on altruistic grounds. He seeks Enlightenment for all sentient beings, and postpones his entry into *nirvāṇa* to lead others to this liberation. During his practice of the six *pāramitā*s or transcendental virtues, he makes four universal vows: (i) to save innumerable sentient beings, (ii) to eradicate earthly desires, (iii) to master immeasurable Buddhist teachings, and (iv) to attain Supreme Enlightenment.

The most widely venerated Bodhisattva in Tibet is the Ṣaḍakṣarī Lokeśvara, who incarnates in the Dalai Lamas to lead people to the bliss of Wisdom and Compassion. His mantra of six syllables *(ṣaḍ-akṣara)* is *OṀ MA-ṆI PA-DME HŪṀ* which is inscribed on the flat surfaces of sturdy rocks. Specific walls are erected to proclaim the *mantra*. Human hands whirl *maṇi* wheels. Lips mutter the incantation and hearts enshrine it.

My father, Professor Raghuvira has explained it as follows:

> *OṀ* is the path and experience of universality.
> *MAṆI* is the jewelline luminosity of the immortal mind.
> *PADME* is its unfolding within the depths of the lotus-centre of the awakened consciousness.
> *HŪṀ* is the ecstasy of breaking
> through bonds and horizons.

> *I invoke the path and experience of universality, so that*
> *the jewelline luminosity of my immortal mind*
> *be unfolded within the depths of the lotus-centre of my*
> *awakened consciousness and I be wafted by*
> *the ecstasy of breaking through*
> *all bonds and horizons.*

Ṣaḍakṣarī Lokeśvara

Ṣaḍakṣarī Lokeśvara (p. 60) is white and emits rays of light, for he is untouched by any imperfection. He has a smiling countenance, as he is filled with compassion for all beings. His eyes look down with tranquility, as he feels equal compassion for all. His two main hands with palms together are in front of the heart indicating the unity of Wisdom and Method. His right hand holds a rosary, a sign that he draws forth beings from the phenomenal existence. His left hand holds a lotus-flower, a sign that he serves living beings but is free from attachment. He is adorned with jewelled ornaments, a sign that while pure he has not abandoned pleasant things. His rays of five colours symbolise that he removes the evils of the six spheres of existence.

The Dalai Lamas are incarnations of Lokeśvara, while the Panchen Lamas are reincarnations of the divine presence of Amitābha, the God of Infinite Light, and the Grand Abbot of the Ganden

Bodhisattva

Bodhisattva means 'Enlightenment-Being' or one who aspires to *bodhi*. In the earliest *Jātaka*s, it means Śākyamuni in his previous lives and in his historic life before his Enlightenment as the Buddha. After the rise of Mahāyāna, Bodhisattva came to mean 'one who seeks and attains Enlightenment for self, but postpones entry into *nirvāṇa* to lead others to this goal.' He generates the aspiration as a vow to achieve Enlightenment for all beings. Then he embarks on the path by practising the Six Perfections *(ṣad-pāramitā)* and the four means to attract beings over aeons. His spiritual progress is divided into several levels *(bhūmi*s*)* in the different *sutra*s. Though he remains in the world, he is not of it. He is not only for personal salvation but carries out altruistic practice. His predominant characteristic is compassion in which he devotes himself to the sufferings of others and leads them to happiness, even at the cost of his life. He makes universal vows before embarking on the Six Perfections that are (1) alms giving, (2) keeping the percepts, (3) forbearance, (4) assiduousness, (5) meditation, and (6) attaining wisdom. Bodhisattvas can be both male and female. There are terrestrial and transcendental Bodhisattvas. Transcendental Bodhisattvas are venerated as showing the way and helping in need. Avalokiteśvara and Mañjuśrī are two of the several important ones.

Monastery (one of the most respected monasteries in Lhasa) incarnates Maitreya of the Tuṣita Heaven.

The *Maṇi Kambum* relates that Amitābha caused a white ray of light to issue from his right eye, which brought the Lokeśvara into existence. He is the measured light of the Moon and Sun, both shown at the top of the *thaṅka,* and the personification of Power. He is the guardian of the Buddhist faith until Maitreya appears on earth. This *thaṅka* represents the unity of Tibet in the personalities of the three supreme incarnations of the three divinities, achieved by the tremendous energy, breadth of vision and astute political action by 'The Great Fifth' Dalai Lama, securing the overall unification of Tibet and by putting the Tsang Incarnate, the Panchen Lama, as the second highest incarnation in the Tibetan hierarchy.

Eleven-headed Avalokiteśvara

The Eleven-headed Avalokiteśvara (p. 63) has eleven heads arranged in five series, in a pyramidal sequence of 3, 3, 3, 1 and 1. The topmost head is that of his origination: Amitābha. 'Those heads looking forward wear an aspect of benevolence, the left ones express anger at the faults of men, while the right faces smile graciously at the good deeds or in scorn at evil-doers.'

ABOVE: *Saḍakṣarī Lokeśvara, flanked by two stupas that represent his two acolytes Maṇidhara and Saḍakṣarī Mahāvidyā (a hypostasis of the six mystic syllables).*

FACING PAGE: *Saḍakṣarī Lokeśvara represents the famous* mantra *of six* (ṣaḍ) *syllables* (akṣara): OṀ MA-ṆI-PA-DME HŪṀ. *The Mani Kambum annals of Tibet say that he is the patron deity of Tibet. As heads of the Tibetan State, the Dalai Lamas are his incarnations. The* mantra *is called* sarva-rājendra *or 'Emperor of all Kings.'*

Legend explains the eleven heads as follows: 'Avalokiteśvara descended into hell, converted the wicked, liberated them, and conducted them to Sukhāvatī, the paradise of his spiritual father, Amitābha. He discovered, however, to his dismay, that for every culprit converted and liberated, another instantly took his place, and legend claims that his head split into ten pieces from grief and despair on discovering the extent of wickedness in the world, and the utter hopelessness of saving all mankind. Amitābha caused each piece to become a head, and placed the heads on the body of Avalokiteśvara and his own image above them all.'

According to the Tibetan master, Mkhas-grub Saṅs-rgyas-ye-śes there is another symbolism for the eleven faces: ten represents the ten *pāramitās*

ABOVE AND FACING PAGE: *The Eleven-headed Avalokiteśvara. The faces of compassion in front look after virtuous beings; three faces of anger on the left deliver evil creatures; three on the right encourage people to enter* dharma; *a single face looks on at the disillusionment of the world, and that on the top preaches Mahayana to lead beings to Enlightenment.*

and the eleventh is the *Dharma-kāya.* White in complexion, he has eight hands: the two central hands are in the *namaskāra-mudrā* of salutation, the three right ones hold a rosary, *cakra, varada,* and the three left ones have a lotus, bow and arrow, and a vase. On the top corners are Mañjuśrī and Maitreya, and at the bottom are Mahākāla, Vajrasattva (centre) and Vajrapāṇi. This Eleven-headed Avalokiteśvara is another epiphany with a thousand hands, with an eye on the palm of each hand, and thus with a thousand eyes.

The hands number one thousand because this aspect of Avalokiteśvara corresponds to the essence of the Thousand Buddhas of the Bhadrakalpa. The two principal hands are joined in *añjali,* to signify that he is identical with the *Dharma-kāya,* the plane of the Absolute, and that in this manner his essence is revealed to others. Only the first eight hands have particular symbols, the other 992 all being in the *varada mudrā.*

Thousand-armed Avalokiteśvara

The palm of each of the thousand hands of the Thousand-armed Avalokiteśvara has an eye to see the sufferings of humankind and to help and illuminate all with the light of wisdom. He is the great Compassion and boundless Wisdom. Each of the forty main arms has a different instrument to save sentient beings. His mind does not stop with the use of one arm but moves from one instrument to another so that all his arms are of the utmost degree of efficiency. When Wisdom Immovable is realised, all the arms dynamise into action. The 960 arms depicted as an aureole in the background of the figure are symbolic of his measureless skillful means. Each of the forty main hands saves from a particular trouble and can be evoked by the suffering person. Thus the sun-disc cures blindness. The hand with the moon-disc is invoked if one suffers from fever and seeks coolness.

Amoghavajra's hymn to the Thousand-armed Avalokiteśvara invokes the Thousand-armed Thousand-powered *(sahasra-vīra)* to grant sway over vast dominions

Cittaviśrāmaṇa Avalokiteśvara

The rays of Your knowledge open the lotus of the mind.
Your rays of morality cool those scorched by defilements.
From your cloud-mass of Love
The downpour of Compassion
Soaks Faith's field and ripens the leaves of the Bodhi.

Cittaviśrāmaṇa Avalokiteśvara (p. 66) casts his compassionate look on suffering beings. He

FACING PAGE: *The Eleven-headed Avalokitésvara with a thousand hands and an eye on each palm. He is the Buddhist metamorphosis of Śiva. He is auspicious, invincible, and purifies the* samsar*ic existence of all beings.*

ABOVE: *Cittaviśrāmaṇa Avalokiteśvara is in the mind* (citta) *of the first* Dharma *Kings of Tibet, Sroṅ-btsan-sgam-po, according to the esoteric visions of the Fifth Dalai Lama. The mind is the creator of* saṁsāra *and also that which is beyond it. All that exists is the luminosity of the mind.*

FACING PAGE: *The Thousand-armed Avalokiteśvara.*

is the deification of the action of the Tathāgata. His right hand is in the *varada-mudrā* of granting boons to devotees, and the left hand holds a red lotus with a long stem. In the chignon is Amitābha, and a deer-skin hangs down his left shoulder. The deer-skin symbolises compassion and identifies Avalokiteśvara. A green nimbus invests his head, and a red aureole radiating golden rays encircles his whole body in keeping with the red colour of his Transcendental Buddha, Amitābha. He transmits positive energy, and calms the restless mind with pure thoughts. He unifies blissful wisdom-energy with non-duality. Apparent reality is nothing more than a representation of our mind, which in its innate nature is pure radiance. The mind imprisoned in the world of experience by its actions has to become the innate radiant mind of independent existence.

Mañjuśrī

Mañjuśri is the Lord of Learning, Vāgīśvara, and also a great Bodhisattva in the *Lotus Sūtra* along with Maitreya. Mañjuśrī has several forms. In his most fundamental form he carries the sword on the right and a *Prajñā-pāramitā* manuscript on the left. With the flaming point of the sword he dissipates darkness among men or cleaves asunder the clouds of ignorance. The manuscript on Transcendental Wisdom confers intelligence, memory, wisdom and eloquence. *Mañju* in his name stands for beautiful, lovely, pleasing, charming, suave; *śrī* is brilliance, radiation, splendour, glory. This painting (p. 71) is a reanimation of the resplendence of the divine in its suave colours and delicate delineation.

Mañjuśrī is the eternally youthful, princely being of wisdom, out to discover the true nature of reality, by the double-edged sword of analytic discrimination, which cuts across delusions. The sword destroys all that stands against Truth, which is the wisdom deeply lodged in the superconscious of each one of us. Symbolically, the sword represents righteousness, justice, equity, love and creativity. He rides a golden-haired lion, the symbol of action and energy. The lion's roar can be heard throughout the universe to awaken beings from drowsiness. His red garment befits the *śṛṅgāra rasa* of the passion that he displays.

Arapacana Mañjuśrī

He is red in complexion and accompanied by four divinities. His smiling face is resplendent like the full moon. He is decked with all kinds of princely ornaments, as he sits on a double lotus in the *vajra-paryaṅka* posture.

Arapacana Mañjuśrī or Pañcākṣara Mañjuśrī (p. 70) is wisdom deified and represents the five *(pañca)* letters *(akṣara)*; '*a*', '*ra*', '*pa*', '*ca*' and '*na*'. In

FACING PAGE: *An intricately detailed portrayal of the Thousand-armed Avalokiteśvara.*

FACING PAGE: *Arapacana Mañjuśrī.*

ABOVE: *Mañjuśrī, the ecstasy of transcendental wisdom, sits on a lion the symbol of this wisdom* (prajñā-pāramitā). *The lion's roar can be heard throughout the universe to awaken beings from drowsiness.*

Mañjuśrī, Charming Grace

Mañjuśrī, 'Charming Grace' is one of the most celebrated Bodhisattvas of Mahāyāna. He is depicted as a young prince, wearing a necklace made of tiger claws, used to protect children. As Prince Charming, he is Mañjuśrī Kumārabhūta—the Eternal Youth, Mañjuśrī. He is mentioned in the early *Prajñā-pāramita sutra*s and thus came to personify wisdom *(prajñā)*. He sits on a lion, and brandishes a sword to cut all intellectual and affectional entanglements to reveal the light of transcendental wisdom. His flaming sword cuts throught the veil of ignorance. He holds a blue lotus that bears a book—the *Prajñā-pāramitā*. He is paired with Samantabhadra who represents compassion *(karuṇā)*. *Prajñā* is intellectual and *karuṇā* is emotional; the former represents identity and the latter multiplicity. In Tibet, great scholars are considered incarnations of Mañjuśrī. Texts of *Mādhyamika* philosophy pay homage to him at the beginning. He is the experience of Enlightenment as manifested in intellectual exposition. In his wrathful form, he is called Yamāntaka—Subduer of the Lord of Death, and is one of the most important *Yidam*s of the Gelukpa denomination. In Tibetan Buddhism, *Yidam*s are an aid in the transformation process of the practitioner to comprehend his or her personality structure. The Fifth Dalai Lama recognised the Qing Emperors of China as emanations of Mañjuśrī. Emperor Qianlong (r. 1736-1795) was initiated into the *tantra*s in 1745 by his Imperial Perceptor, Rol-paḥi-rdo-rje. Rol-paḥi-rdo-rje accompanied the Emperor on regular pilgrimages to the Wū-t'ai-shan Mountain dedicated to Mañjuśrī. Even Chairman Mao Tse-tung went to Wū-t'ai-shan to pay homage to Mañjuśrī before taking oath of office in Beijing.

his right hand, he carries the sword of transcendental knowledge to cleave the knotty points and remove the veil of ignorance. In his left hand he holds an Indian style book of the *Prajñā-pāramitā,* the scripture of transcendental wisdom, placed on a full-blown lotus-flower symbolising purity rising above the turbid waters of existence. The left hand is in the *vitarka-mudrā* of disputation. He is whitish-red in colour, and seated in the adamantine posture called the *vajra-paryaṅka.* He is accompanied by four deities: Sūryaprabha, Candraprabha, Keśinī and Upakeśinī in the four corners. The pentad originates from the five syllables *'a', 'ra', 'pa', 'ca', 'na'.* This is the most widely spread form of Mañjuśrī, found as far as Indonesia.

Atīśa, one of the noblest Indian teachers in Tibet is an incarnation of Mañjuśrī. Tsoṅ-kha-pa, the founder of the Gelukpa School, is likewise Mañjuśrī incarnate. As the tutelary deity of astrology, Mañjuśrī is invoked at the beginning of horoscopes for blessings.

White Amoghapāśa

White Amoghapāśa (p. 75) has eight arms. He stands gracefully on a lotus, with a flowing dhoti, and the six usual ornaments. His four right hands hold the rosary, a three-pronged staff *(tridaṇḍī),* and show gestures of charity and reassurance. In the four left hands the attributes are a manuscript, a noose *(pāśa),* a lotus and a spouted waterpot *(kamaṇḍalu).* He is one of the most popular Buddhist deities in Nepal. One of the eight tutelary deities of the Valley, he is frequently represented in sculptures and paintings. Paintings of Amoghapāśa were created to bring long life, prosperity and ample progeny to the donor. He is invoked by the imprisoned and the childless.

Amoghapāśa casts his net in the wilderness of evil passions and catches the 'birds' or beings who transmigrate through the six realms. He drops the noose of beneficial birth into the *saṁsar*ic ocean of suffering and catches the 'fishes' or beings who are sinking to its obscure depths. The noose is the symbol of his original vow to pull all beings to the shore of Awakening.

Red Amoghapāśa

Red Amoghapāśa (p. 74) is flanked by Tārā and Bhṛkuṭī on the right and the left, respectively. The young and gentle Sudhana and the fierce Hayagrīva kneel at the bottom of the pedestal supporting the lotus on which stands Amoghapāśa. He has eight hands. The right hands have a rosary, a three-pronged staff, the *mudrā* of exposition of *Dharma,* and the *varada-mudrā* of munificence. The left hands display the scripture, the lotus,

ABOVE: *Red Amoghapāśa is the main deity of* aṣṭamī-vrata *or the sabbath on the eighth day. The 28 boxed illustrations around the central rectangle represent the 20 merits and 8 blessings that accrue from reciting a hymn to him.*

FACING PAGE: *White Amoghapāśa.*

the noose and the *mudrā* of granting boons. The goddesses are four-armed. Tārā means the Saviouress and Bhṛkuṭī means the Yellow Goddess who frowns. Her three hands hold a rosary, a trident and a vase. The fourth hand is in the *varada mudrā* of munificence.

Rites to Red Amoghapāśa ensure rain, on which depends the prosperity and abundance of Nepal, where agriculture is dominant. Usually the king participates in the rites. The chronicles of the kingdom of Patan mention regular donations to the temples of Red Amoghapāśa at Patan and Bungamati for the celebration of the festival.

On the devotional level, Amoghapāśa symbolises the ability to save all sentient beings with his unfailing and never-in-vain *(amogha)* noose *(pāśa)*. His noose of compassion is the all-embracing four virtues as *upāya*s (means) that lead all beings to Enlightenment, as explained in the *Mahāvairocana Sūtra*. He too casts his net of mercy across the wilderness of evil passions and saves the birds or transmigrating sentient beings.

Hayagrīva

Hayagrīva in his wrathful esoteric form is red in body, has three faces, each face with three eyes—green on the right, red in the centre and whitish on the left, three horse-heads rising out of dishevelled hair over his heads. The first face is smiling, the central face shows an upturned tongue, and in the left face he bites his lips. He has six arms: on the right they hold from top to bottom—a *vajra*, a *khaṭvāṅga* (skull-staff), and a sword; on the left the first hand is in a threatening *mudrā*, followed by two others holding an arrow and a noose made of human guts. His eight feet trample on eight snakes. He has snakes for ornaments and is clad in tiger-skin.

He represents the cutting away of the defilement of the mind, to see delusion as other than awakening. He symbolises the virtue of severance by his wrathful form. Buddhaguhya in his commentary on the *Mahāvairocana Sūtra* says that Hayagrīva is called 'Horse-head' because the speed with which he purifies and destroys the defilement of the mind is like that of a galloping horse.

FACING PAGE: *Hayagrīva in his wrathful form, from the popular manual for meditation on him by the Panchen Lama. He was popular with the horse-loving Tibetans and Mongols. Buddhaguhya's commentary on the* Mahāvairocana Sutra *says that he purifies the defilements of the mind with the speed of a galloping horse.*

Goddesses

As the Bodhisattva Gautama became the Buddha, the Enlightened One, he touched the Earth, the Impartial Mother of all, as witness to his Enlightenment. Sthāvarā, the Earth Goddess, emerged from the ground and said: 'You are enlightened. I am the eye-witness.' The evil Māra discouraged, his heart bleeding from a secret wound, wrote on the ground: 'Gautama has destroyed my empire.'

The goddesses dissolve the whirlwinds of phenomena into active life. They convey the multi-layered mind-body continuum of corporeality, cognitivity and spirituality, subtly interwoven and mutually interactive. The *Caṇḍa-mahāroṣaṇa Tantra* urges with impassioned conviction:

> Women are heaven, women are truth,
> Women are the supreme fires of transformation.
> Women are Buddha,
> Women are religious community,
> Women are the perfection of wisdom.

Aṣṭamaṅgala Devī

Aṣṭamaṅgala Devī (p. 82), the Four-faced Goddess of Eight Auspicious Emblems, holds the wheel, lotus, conch and the banner of victory in the four right hands, and the *śrīvatsa* (the endless knot), a pair of gold fish, a vase and a royal umbrella in the four left hands. The Wheel of the Law recalls the first sermon of Śākyamuni at the Deer Park at Sarnath. Worshipped from the earliest Buddhist period, it has cosmological and imperial associations. It is the world-controlling solar disc. As an emblem of sovereignty it is associated with the empowerment of high-ranking Lamas. The wheel is a symbol of activity (energy). The lotus is the divine seat and symbolic dominion, besides epitomising purity and the transcendental state of Enlightenment. The white conch symbolises the spoken word. As a Tathāgata sounds it, the damned in hell who perceive its sound are liberated and go to the Tuṣita Heaven. The umbrella connotes the universal spiritual domain. The *śrīvatsa* is the interrelatedness of all things and the unending interaction between wisdom and compassion. It also connotes longevity. The twin fish, shown with arching bodies, are symbolic of obstacle-free freedom, and the life-giving properties of water. The two goldfish are the symbols of the means *(upāya)* and wisdom *(prajñā)*. The vase contains life-giving water and symbolises longevity. As a container of treasure it symbolises the ideal riches of *Dharma* and the fulfilment of aspirations. The banner of victory conveys spiritual sway.

White Tārā

White Tārā (p. 83) has seven eyes: three on the forehead, two on the palms and another two on the soles. Pure of being, having perceived the Nature of Emptiness *(śūnyatā)* like dreams, illusions and mirages, the devotee visualises the letter *'A'*, transforming into a moon disc. Upon it he visualises the white syllable TĀṀ (for Tārā), as a collection of white light-rays. These rays spread in all directions, purify all sentient beings, and assume the form of Tārā, with the body of a sixteen-year old, decked with all ornaments, her right hand in the *varada-mudrā* of charity and the left holding a white lotus in full-bloom. Her abundant hair is held by a crown. She is smiling and graceful, and of moon white brightness. She is the Saviouress par excellence. The Tibetan name *sgrol,* like its original Sanskrit *Tārā,* means to cross over (root: *tar*) the Ocean of Existence. She is invoked to save mankind from the perils threatening it. Tārā, the kinetic power of compassion *(karuṇā),* saves *(tārayati)* suffering creatures.

In the daily ritual practices of the most important monasteries, the meditation on the *maṇḍala* of Tārā takes place at seven in the morning. Sitting on a lotus-seat of strong striving, on a lotus with roots of aspiration, firm in the ground of fully developed faith, the divine Tārā cools with compassion, while her smiling face spreads uncontaminated bliss, so says the hymn of Mātṛceṭa in its Tibetan rendering.

The translucent colours of the delicate brush of a devotee kiss with heavenly lines, White Tārā, blooming with youth, with the beauty of a million autumn moons. She is all-beautiful who steals from the sun and moon their light. Her sapphire tresses are half-knotted on top and the rest fall freely over the shoulders. Radiant as the eternal snows, her right hand is in the *mudrā* of supreme giving, her boundless generosity that ensures eight *siddhis* and Supreme Enlightenment. Graceful and calm, her left hand holds a blue lotus, the symbol of protection from all terrors and fears. As refuge of the world, the eyes on her hands and feet lead sentient creatures to the isle of blissful liberation. She sits on a white lotus indicative of fully developed compassion and knowledge. Her coronet, earrings, necklaces, armbands, bracelets, anklets and belt sparkle in their celestial elegance. She grants immaculate wisdom, learning, contemplation and meditation.

Green Tārā

Syāma Tārā or Green Tārā (p. 86) is kissed by the colour of gold, as she descends into the heart of the devotee from her heavenly heights. She can be recognised by her posture of sitting in the *lalitāsana* with her hanging right foot resting on a lotus. The *vitarka-mudrā* of disputation holding a blue lotus *(utpala)* above the shoulder is also characteristic of her. The goddess is seated on a lotus, while a small figure of Amitāyus above signifies her spiritual

ABOVE: *White Tārā blooming with youth, with the beauty of a million autumn moons, carries devotees across the ocean of* samsar*ic existence* (bhava-sāgara), *beyond all becoming.*

FACING PAGE: *Aṣṭamaṅgalā Devī represents protection (umbrella), unhampered emancipation (golden fish), sacred hymns (conch), purity (lotus), constant evolution (wheel), victory (banner), riches (vase), and devotion (endless knot). She guards us against evil forces, and causes the body, speech and mind to blossom like the waxing moon.*

Kanjur

The *Kanjur* is the canonical collection of Tibetan Buddhist scriptures. The word means translated *(jur,* written *gyur)* instructions *(kan,* written *bkaḥ)* of the Buddha. It comprises over a hundred volumes and contains translations of more than a thousand *sutra*s and *tantra*s from Sanskrit originals. They are faithful renderings and hence of great value when original Indian texts in Sanskrit have been lost. Bu-ston (AD 1290-1364) edited the two massive collections of the *Kanjur* and *Tanjur,* which contain the literary and spiritual heritage of Buddhism. The redaction was done at Zhalu and Narthang Monasteries in Tibet. The *Tanjur* contains commentaries, glosses and other secondary works, besides secular works on medicine, metallurgy, dictionaries, grammar, poetry, logic, philosophical systems, lyrics, dramas, etc. The *Kanjur* is divided into six sections: 1. *Tantra,* 2. *Prajñā-pāramitā,* 3. *Ratnakūṭa,* 4. *Avataṁsaka,* 5. *Sutra* (Hīnayāna and Mahāyāna), 6. *Vinaya.*

The codification of the greatest collections of Buddhist scriptures was a work of generations. The monks of Narthang Monastery in Tibet gathered the sacred texts with great zeal. They were helped by Ḥjam-dbyaṅs, the chaplain of Buyantu, who sent a large sum of money to place the Canon in the temples of Narthang. Bu-ston started his revision from the Narthang collection. He alludes to the pious patronage of Buyantu for the first Tibetan codification of the scriptures. The Narthang collection became the common source for successive editions.

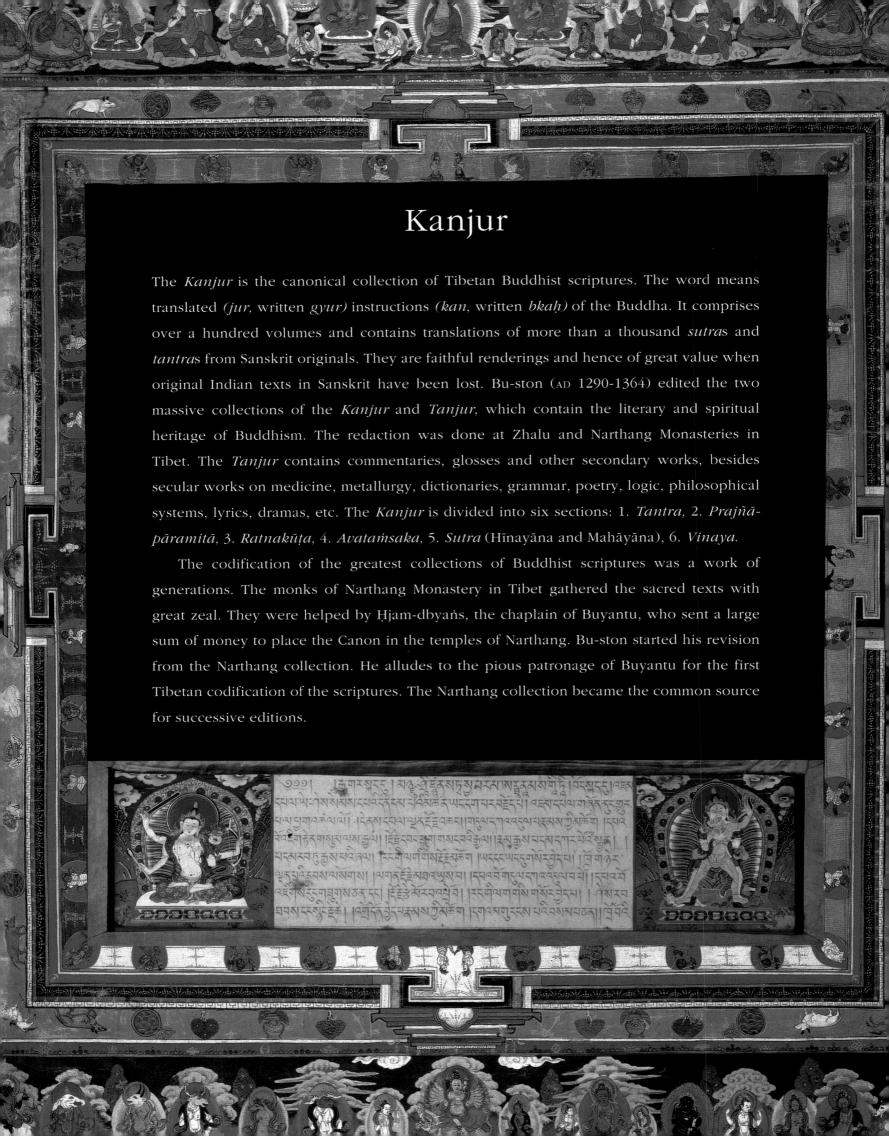

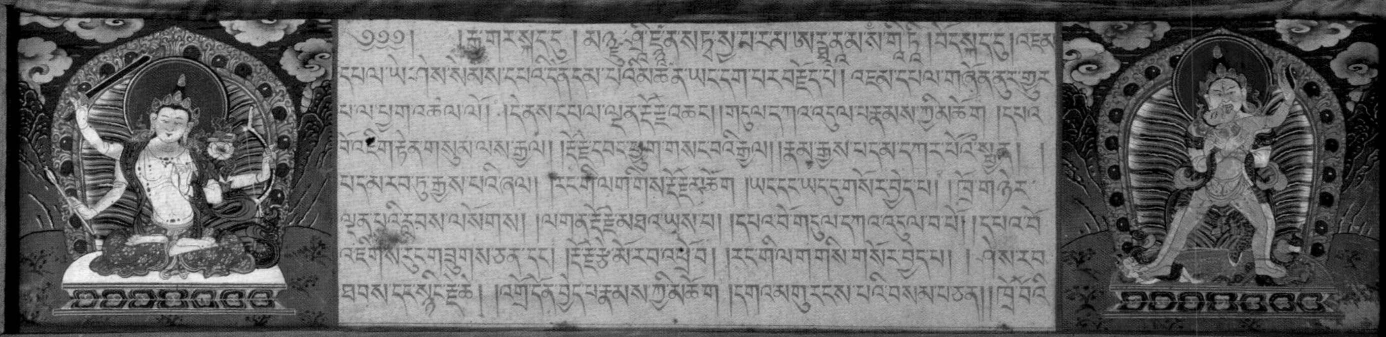

ABOVE: *White Tārā brings happiness, virtue and peace.*

descent and the mystical plane to which she belongs. Her right hand is in the *varada-mudrā* of granting a boon, while her left hand is in the attitude of protection holding a lotus by its long stem.

The Indian teacher, Nāgārjuna gives a detailed interpretation of Green Tārā in his work in the Tanjur: 'The goddess has a single face because the global knowledge of things is gnosis. The green colour points to the power of performing every kind of action. Green is, in fact, also the colour of Amoghasiddhi, a Buddha of the supreme pentad who presides over action. Of her two hands, the one on the right is the symbol of the relative or conventional truth, and the one on the left is the symbol of the Transcendental or Absolute Truth. Her right leg is stretched because the gnosis symbolised by Tārā implies the renunciation of all kinds of sin. Her left leg is bent towards her body because this gnosis realises every kind of virtue. Her ornaments signify the perfection of knowledge and moral praxis. Her right hand is in the attitude of gifting implying that the perfection of liberality *(dāna-pāramitā)* should be a companion of gnosis; her left hand is in the attitude of protection because it protects creatures from all kinds of fear. She holds the lotus in order to show that from her all beings, taking refuge in her, derive their blessedness. She is conceived of as being sixteen-year-old (the years of eternal youth, *kiśorī*) because she has the power to realise the welfare of all. She sits on a seat as white as the moon, because she is consubstantial with mystic knowledge. This seat leans over a double lotus *(viśvapadma)* because this mystical knowledge is accompanied by compassion, the other indissoluble coefficient of the thought of illumination.'

Sarasvatī

Sarasvatī (p. 90) is Dbyaṅs-can-ma in Tibetan. Sarasvatī is the Flowing-One, the Goddess of Eloquence, of Wisdom, the Mother of Speech expressing herself in creative action. She is the transcendental word, the power and grace of Brahmā, the Immense Being, playing on the lyrical *vīṇā*. She is the goddess absolute who enhances the intuitive knowledge of the initiate. She translates intellective knowledge into an inward psychic experience. Though sunk in ignorance, humankind carries within the divine spark, which is celestial nature itself, the purest light.

Eyebrows like a crescent moon, the eyes gazing and encompassing the world, round cheeks and chin, a bridged nose, clear skin—the whole body of the goddess is suffused with tender enchantment. The Fifth Dalai Lama recalls in a hymn to her the divine charm of the goddess who quenches earth's thirst like rain-clouds.

FACING PAGE: *Green Tārā is the intuitive vision to know the ultimate reality through her* darśana *or visualisation. She tramples under her feet the enemies of the higher mind, and saves devotees from all disasters.*

She marks victory for overcoming one's spiritual shortcomings from within. She disperses the black clouds of ignorance to reveal the radiance of learning and spirituality, to triumph over failings, so that pure gold shines brighter in the fire of *saṁsāra*.

Uṣṇīṣavijayā

Uṣṇīṣavijayā (pgs. 92, 93), or Gtsug-tor-rnam-rgyal-ma in Tibetan, is also known as Vijayā (Tibetan: Rnam-rgyal-ma). She is a personification of the *Uṣṇī ṣavijayā-dhāraṇī*. Her eight arms hold:

(Right hands)
Buddha on lotus;
arrow;
This pair of hands holds a *viśva-vajra* noose in the *tarjanī-mudrā* of threatening and the other hand is in the *varada-mudrā*.

(Left hands)
abhaya mudrā of granting fearlessness;
bow filled vessel with aśoka branch.

One of the most popular goddesses of Tibet, she is white in complexion, in the prime of youth and wears varied ornaments. Her hair is tied in a high chignon and she holds an image of Vairocana in her crown. She is three-headed, each one of them with three

ABOVE: *A stunning gilded bronze sculpture of Green Tārā by the first patriarch of Mongolia the Great Saint Zanabazar* (Jñānavajra) *Ündür Gegen (AD 1635-1723), at the height of his creative genius.*

FACING PAGE: *Green Tārā as an appliqué* thaṅka. *She redeems devotees from the bubble-like existence and leads humans across the boundless ocean of being, as the devotees invokes her to liberate them from the fleeting breeze of transience.*

eyes. The three faces are yellow, white, and blue: all sweet in expression. Many hymns are devoted to her in the collection of divine visualisations entitled *Sādhanamālā*.

Vasudhārā

Vasudhārā (p. 95) is the flowing *(dhārā)* of bounty *(vasu)*, the plenitude of wealth, the stream of riches. With the shower of jewels and pearls, affluence and lucrative deals, she amply rewards her pious worshippers in an endless flood of fortune. She radiates happiness and sits gracefully in the *lalitāsana* posture with her right foot resting on a lotus. She is of golden complexion, in the prime of youth and decked with ornaments. She has six arms. Her right hands exhibit the *namaskāra-mudrā* of salutation, the *varada-mudrā* of bestowing charity, and the ears of corn. The left hands hold a book, a sheaf of corn and an auspicious vessel containing jewels. Her four attributes—the gesture of charity, the auspicious pot, the gems and the sheaf of grain signify her role as the giver of wealth. As the Goddess of Wealth, Vasudhārā is very popular. Innumerable images and paintings indicate that she has been a household deity. Her adoration is accompanied by narration of episodes from the story of Sucandra, which emphasizes the importance of worshipping the goddess.

The five protective goddesses, or Pañcarakṣā are placed in the innermost yard of her *maṇḍala*. In the surrounding second yard are representations of the Eight Guardians of the Directions *(dikpāla)*. The three concentric squares of the *maṇḍala* are enclosed by four portals within thick ramparts. Elaborate with festoons, the four portals cover the four cardinal directions. Their decorative complexity and richness of design is rendered in fine details. Beyond the three squares and the surrounding bastion-like walls with their four elaborate gateways, are three circles of the psychosphere—the circles of lotuses, *vajras* and fire (from inside to outside).

Kurukullā

Red Kurukullā (p. 96) has four hands: the original pair of hands holds a bow and arrow while the lower two hands hold a goad and noose, all made of flowers. With the upper pair she shoots a blue-lotus arrow; her lower right holds a hook and the corresponding left, a snare. She has three eyes and protruding teeth, which give her a ferocious appearance. She resides on the Kurukullā Mountain in Lāṭadeśa in Gujarat (western India), whence her name. Her eyes are red and injected with blood. Her tawny erect hair is encircled by a diadem of five skulls. She has the appearance of a young girl of sixteen years. Her body is covered with ornaments

FACING PAGE: *Sarasvatī delights human beings with beautiful sounds and delicate expressions. The first syllable* 'SA' *comprises* 'S', *'solidity', and* 'A', *'no solidity'. As her words are 'not solid' she makes humans understand impermanence and at the same time she makes them experience the 'solid' essence of the Tathāgata.*

ABOVE AND FACING PAGE: *Uṣṇīṣavijayā or the Goddess of Supreme Victory washes away lifetimes of karmic sediment. A Sakyapa prayer invokes her:*

Pacify all karmic and emotional impurities
With the samādhi of supreme, stainless bliss.
May you wash away and purify all that
With a stream of immortal nectar.

made from bones and countless jewels. She dances with the right leg raised. Her left leg is placed on a prostrate male figure. Though portrayed in a terrifying aspect, she is the Goddess of Love. The face has a haughty expression, contorted to a smirk. She is the Buddhist counterpart of Kāmadeva, the God of Love, and his consort Rati. She is dancing on the bodies of Kāmadeva and Rati lying on Rāhu. Her dishevelled hair seem to fly about her face. Wrapped around her waist is a tiger skin, and a garland of severed human heads hangs around her neck. She has a red aureole behind her. Amitābha sits on the top in the centre. In the fullness of youth, she displays amorous sentiments. She is ready to shoot a flowery arrow from a flowery bow to strike love. If a devotee wants to win a woman, he should meditate, beginning with the first date of the bright fortnight, thrice a day, on an image of the divine goddess, wearing red garments. With a joyful heart and with firm intent, he should recite her mantra: *Oṁ kurukulle hrīḥ amukīṁ me vaśam ānaya svāhā.*

When a myriad recitations have been completed, the desired one, smitten by Cupid, appears without robes and in the agony of love.

Vajravārāhī

Vajravārāhī (p. 98) is red like the pomegranate flower. She is two-armed. She exhibits in her right hand the *vajra* along with the raised index finger, and shows in the left the cranium and the *khaṭvāṅga* (skull-staff). She is one-faced and three-eyed, has dishevelled hair, is marked with the six auspicious symbols and is nude. She is the essence of the five kinds of knowledge, and is the embodiment of *sahaja* pleasure. Envision the beings of the three realms (subterranean, terrestrial, celestial) as the *maṇḍala* and all of them as enjoying great bliss. Having experienced bliss, the heroes and heroines of the three outer realms dissolve into the eight great cremation grounds, and the cremation grounds dissolve into the measureless mansion, which dissolves into the four innermost *yoginīs*: Khaṇḍarohā (adolescent), Rūpiṇī (blooming belle), Rāmā (enchanting beauty), and Ḍākinī (queen charmer).

Vajrayoginī

Vajrayoginī (p. 99) is Enlightenment spontaneously appearing in an embodied form. She is blood red in colour and has loose flowing black hair. She is dancing, wears bone ornaments, and brandishes a skull-cup brimming with ambrosia. She is beautiful, passionate and untamed. She tramples corpses underfoot. She stands in the *ālīḍha* posture on the orb of the sun, and is in the prime of youth. She insists that all female beings in the universe

FACING PAGE: *Vasudhārā is the divine manifestation of prosperity, abundance and affluence. She is accompanied by eight* yakṣiṇīṣ. *She sits in the noble attitude, is graceful and youthful, and is crowned by Ratnasambhava.*

are her embodiments or manifestations, and thus should be respected, honoured, and served without exception. She takes form so that women, seeing Enlightenment in the female form, will recognise their innate divinity and potential for Enlightenment. Devotion to her should be expressed as respect for women, while respect for women provides a way of measuring devotion to the goddess. She promises her blessings to a man who worships her.

Ramatī

Rematī (p. 100) is maroon in colour and has two arms: the right holds a sword and the left a wealth-producing mongoose. The mongoose is a key to her identification. In ancient times, purses were made by stitching up the skin of a mongoose *(nakula);* whence we have the term *nakulaka* for money-bag or purse in Buddhist works. Rematī is derived from *rai* or 'property, possessions, wealth, riches'. Revatī in the plural means 'the wealthy one' or 'the shining one'. Rematī with outstretched *vajra*-wings has a body of dark-brown colour, holds a sword and a skull-cup, while a mongoose rests in the crook of her left arm. Yakṣī Rematī holds a sword in her right hand and a treasure-producing mongoose in her left, but her colour is black.

The goddess Ma-gcig Rdo-rje-rab-brtan-ma is pictured as a dark-brown or blood-coloured goddess with one head, riding on a cross-breed between a mule and a wild ass. Her right hand brandishes a flaming *rākṣasa*-sword, and the left one holds a skull-cup filled with the blood of enemies and obstacle-creating demons. The colour of her body is the same as that of Lha-mo, who is the manifestation of different concepts. Her left hand holds a skull-cup and not a mongoose. As goddesses of life and death, of fecundity and destruction, they are the flow of cosmic Becoming. They are one in their real essence in the highest degrees of esoteric contemplation. A large number of chthonian feminine deities have merged in the several forms of Dpal-ldan Lha-mo.

Dpal-ldan Lha-mo

She (pgs. 102, 103) rides a mule and is of dark blue colour. She is the manifestation of different concepts and an assimilation of a number of goddesses under several skies. A hymn to the goddess, eulogises her as Rematī, as Dmag-zor-ma, as a defender of the teachings, who overpassed many valleys where there are no herbs, no water, no trees, but tiring desert plains, high and terrible mountains, snow storms, wild beasts and where resound the cries of many demons and birds.

She has one face and two hands. In the right she brandishes a sandalwood club marked by a *vajra,*

FACING PAGE: *Kurukullā is all red in love. She is invoked by lovers for her power of bewitching men and women by shooting floral arrows from her floral bow.*

ABOVE: *Vajravārāhī is the essence of the five kinds of knowledge, the embodiment of innate pleasure, as she dances in the sphere of phenomena in a land of stainless purity. She represents the egalitarian vision, the gynocentric balance that has blazed at the core of Tantric Buddhism. Kurukullā adorned with various ornaments, passionate in expression, proud of her blossoming youth, she shoots a floral arrow strung on a floral bow. She is the counterpart of Kāmadeva and his consort Rati.*

FACING PAGE: *Vajrayoginī insists on a female form. Women should be respected, honoured and served as her embodiments. A man who worships them will gain her blessings. She is the self-illuminating wisdom in the palace of Enlightenment.*

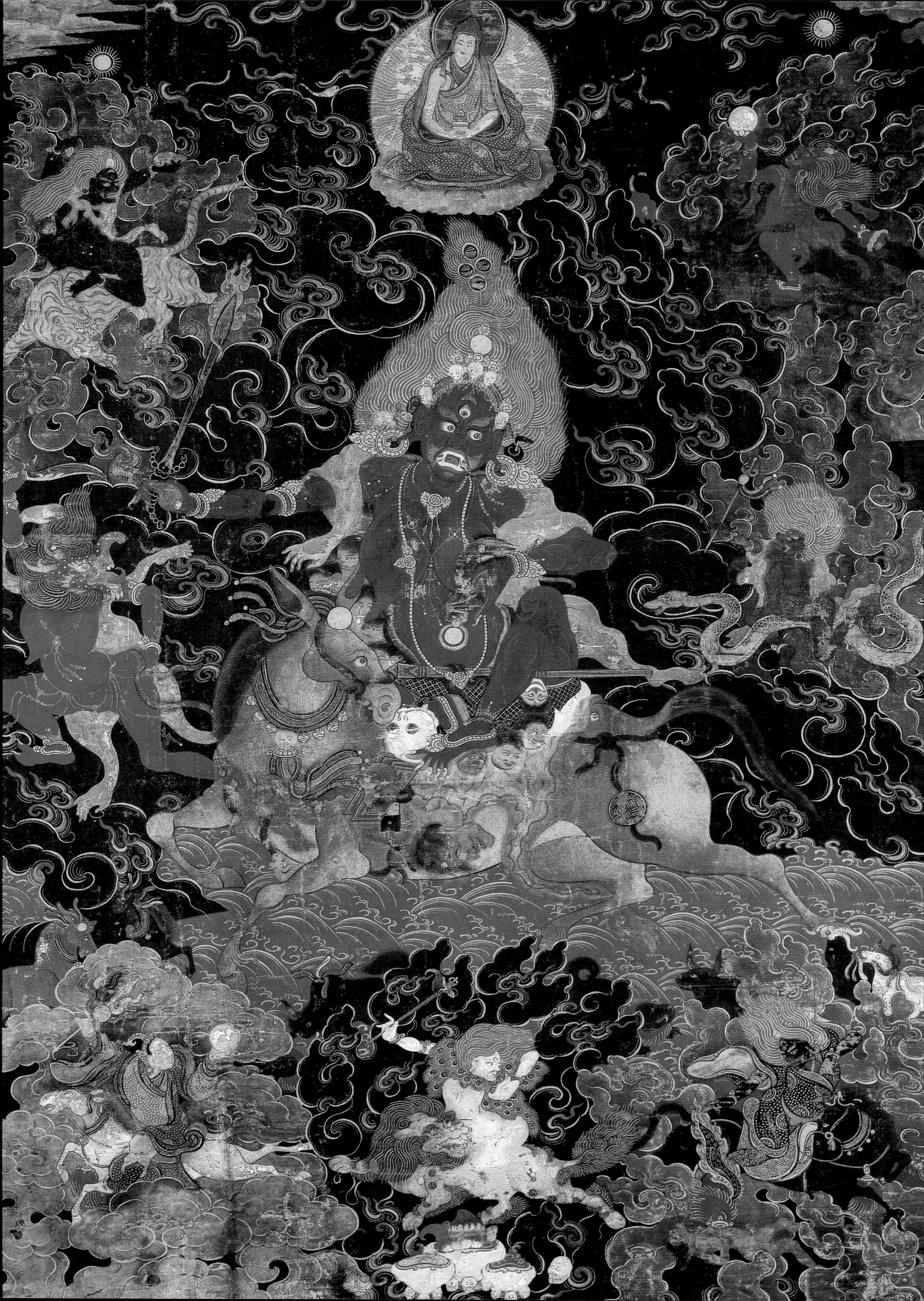

high on the head of those who have forsaken the vows. Her left hand is tightly held against the breast with a skull full of blood. She is terrific with her sharp teeth, and laughs with a thunderous noise. With three red frowning eyes, flaming red like lightning, and eyelashes flaming like the cosmic fire at the end of aeons, she has a diadem made of five human skulls. She wears a flowing scarf of black silk and has a girdle of snakes. The hair on her head stand on ends, and above them is a panoply of peacock feathers. She rides in the middle of a vast wild sea of blood and fat, amidst raging black storms. Her mount is a wild ass with a belt of demon heads, and the skin of demons as cover and the reins are of poisonous snakes. She emanates from the syllable *'BHYO'*. A multitude appears as her train, brandishing various weapons such as thunderbolts, choppers, swords, hatchets, hooks and poles to impale criminals, while a fiercely blazing fire dominates the scene. The prevailing terrific aspect is the beatific power vanquishing negative forces, which are psychic activities that bind us to the cycle of life and death. She assumes a terrific aspect to combat evil forces; thus is Dmag-zor-ma, the one overpowering and crushing the host of passions. She vanquishes spiritual demons as well as the demoniac enemies.

Lha-mo is flanked by blue Makaravaktrā and red Siṁhavaktrā. She is surrounded by the four goddesses of the four seasons: rain, spring, autumn and winter. They can be distinguished by their skirts of leaves and feathers. They are known in Tibetan as Dus-bzhiḥi lha-mo. Dominating the lower part of the *thaṅka* (p. 103) is Rdo-rje-kun-tu-bzaṅ, riding a lion, with a *vajra* aloft in her right hand and a flask in the left resting on her thigh astride the lion. She is the first of the cycle of the Twelve Bstan-sruṅ-ma or indigenous goddesses admitted into the train of Lha-mo, as the guardians of the new spiritual order. These twelve goddesses can be depicted in wrathful or peaceful forms.

Lho-mo was worshipped by the Sakyapas whence she passed to the Gelukpas, whose great master Dge-ḥdun-grub made her the guardian deity of the Ganden Monastery, one of the four major monasteries of Lhasa with political authority and great sanctity in the Lamaist world. The Fifth Dalai Lama detailed her rites. The goddess was worshipped across Tibet and in Mongolia, in big monasteries and private chapels.

Five Long-Life Goddesses

The Five Long-life Goddesses (p. 104) are known as Tshe-riṅ mched lṅa in Tibetan. They are ancient Tibetan mountain goddesses who were won over by Padmasambhava, and bound by oath to the Buddhist *Dharma*. At the foot of the Jo-mo-gaṅs-

FACING PAGE: *Dpal-ldan Lha-mo is accessible in the highest degree of meditation. She was the guardian deity of the Ganden Monastery, one of the four major monasteries of Lhasa which held political and religious sway in the Lamaist world.*

ABOVE AND FACING PAGE: *Dpal-ldan Lha-mo or Rematī is the first among the eight protective deities known as drag-śad brgyad. She is the wild and energetic figure of Tibetan grasslands, who vanquishes the destructive forces of egotism. She appears at the Lake Lhampo Latso, 90 miles south-east of Lhasa. This magic lake reveals reflections of the future on its surface.*

dkar Mountain are five glacial lakes with water of different colours believed to represent the goddesses. Their worship is common among the Gelukpas and a chapel is dedicated to them on the upper floor of the Jo-khang, the main cathedral of Lhasa. Their worship is conducted in a lonely but lovely wood blooming with flowers. Besides offerings of food and drinks, special offerings of medicine, bronze mirror, crystal, spotless turquoise, to name afew objects, are made.

The chief deity of this group is Bkra-śis-tshe-riṅ-ma. Her body is white in colour. She smiles, but is apt to change within a moment into an angry mood. She has two hands and one face with three eyes. In her right hand she brandishes a nine-pointed vajra of gold, while in her left hand she holds a vessel full of *amṛta* (nectar), in front of her heart. Her mount is a white lioness. The place in front of the chief deity is assigned to the blue goddess Mthiṅ-gi-zhal-bzaṅ-ma. She holds a magic mirror and a white stick with streamers. A wild ass with sapphire-blue hair and a white muzzle is her mount. On the right side appears the yellow goddess Blo-bzaṅ-ma. With her right hand she holds a vessel filled with choice food, while her left hand rests in the manner of bestowing gifts. She rides on a tiger with golden hair. Behind her is the red goddess Cod-pan-mgrin-bzaṅ-ma. With her right hand she holds a chest filled with various kinds of jewels, and the left one lifts a gem. She rides a hind with coral-red hair. On the left resides the green goddess Gtad-dkar-ḥgro-bzaṅ-ma. She holds a bushel of *dūrvā* grass and a snake-snare. Her mount is a turquoise-green dragon. All these five goddesses wear dresses of various kinds of silk, and ornaments of gold, turquoise, jewels, for instance.

FACING PAGE: *The Five Long-life Goddesses are known as 'sisters', implying the interconnectedness of their roles. They represent five co-ordinates of a hale and hearty life endowed with beauty, wise counsel, jewelline mind, and noble demeanour. Together they are the joy and essence of life as an instrument of* dharma *or values.*

Tantras and Maṇḍalas

Tantra means 'weave, weft, continuum' of the systems of meditation, ritual and fruition, transmitted from master to disciple. The lineage is important for the authenticity of the spiritual development of the practitioner. Hence the term '*tantra*' is an emphasis on the continuity of transmission. *Tantras* were expounded by the Buddha in his *Dharma-kāya* manifestation and not in his historic person. They describe spiritual development in terms of ground, path and fruition. The ground is the practitioner, the path is meditation that purifies the ground, and fruition is the final state of Tantric practice. There are two kinds of *tantras*: ones oriented on the concept of light, and the others on sexual symbology. The latter comprise the *Supreme Yoga Tantras*, and seek transcendence of the duality of the masculine principle and the feminine principle through their union.

Phototropic or Outer Tantras

Historical evolution of the *tantras* leads to a two-fold classification: (i) Phototropic or *Outer Tantras*, and (ii) Erototropic or *Inner Tantras* according to the Nyingmapa sect. *Outer Tantras* or Phototropic *Tantras* are dominated by the concept of light. The *pañca-raśmi*—the five luminous elements—are at the basis of cosmic evolution, supreme reality or 'essential light'. The central Tathāgata of the three classes of *tantras* are epiphanies of light: Amitābha in the *Kriyā Tantras*; Vairocana in the *mudrā* of Amitābha in the *Caryā Tantras*; Vairocana in the *Bodhyagrī mudrā* in the *Yoga Tantras*. Amitābha is 'Infinite Light'; Vairocana is 'Effulgence'. The phototropic evolution shows three stages whose main Tathāgatas are Amitābha, Rocana *(Avataṁsaka Sūtras)*, and Vairocana (in several *tantras*). The *Gaṇḍavyūha* has a list of Tathāgatas, beginning with Maitreya, and ending with Abhyuccadeva or Rocana, designating the trans-historical, symbolic Supreme Being. The Buddha shifts from an individual to a cosmic principle, and is the highest *(abhyucca)* Divine Being *(deva)*. That Rocana and Abhyuccadeva used synonymously point to a stage when Rocana had evolved as the highest Tathāgata leading to Vairocana of the *Caryā Tantras*. He wears a crown, and has both hands in the *dhyāna-mudra*. Tibetans refer to him as Abhisambodhi-Vairocana. Vairocana of the Vajradhātu realm has a crown of the Five Tathāgatas and is distinguished by his unique *bodhyagrī-mudrā*.

Erototropic or Inner Tantras

These *tantras* go back to Vajradhara, Vajrasattva and Akṣobhya. From the Akṣobhya tradition evolved the deities of *Anuttara Yoga,* coupled in the *Yab-Yum.* Sukhāvatī, the western paradise of Amitābha, is devoid of women, while Abhirati, the eastern paradise of Akṣobhya, has beauties, involving orgiastic traditions. The evolution of Akṣobhya to the *Yab-Yum* figures was a natural course.

The Akṣobhya tradition evolved into the *Inner Tantras* with their emphasis on the *yoginī* or *ḍākinī.* The tantric female or *yoginī* was characterised by proud self-assurance and physical robustness. *Ḍākinī,* the feminine form of *ḍāka,* can be traced to Tamil where it refers to 'strength'. The role of women in the emergence of the *Anuttara Yoga Tantras* with their *Yab-Yum* images was a development of *strī-ratna* in Akṣobhya's Abhirati paradise.

The cults of Amitābha and Akṣobhya were collateral as their paradises of the west and east were natural pairs. The first extant Chinese translations of the *Sukhāvatī-vyūha* and *Akṣobhya-vyūha* were done simultaneously by Laugākṣin in AD 180.

The *Inner Tantras* or the *Supreme Yoga (Anuttara Yoga) Tantras* are classified in the Derge woodprint edition of the Tibetan Canon (Kanjur) as follows:

(i) Neither *Yogī* nor *Yoginī Tantra*: Kālacakra

(ii) *Yoginī Tantras*: Heruka, Saṁvara, Hevajra, Vajrakīla, Mahākāla

(iii) *Yogī Tantras*: Guhyasamāja, Vajrapāṇi, Yamāntaka, Vajrabhairava, Vajradhara.

The sequence of the Derge Kanjur has been followed in the ensuing pages.

Kālacakra

The Kālacakra (pgs. 112, 113) was revealed, according to tradition, by the Buddha twelve months after his Enlightenment in the *stūpa* of Dhānyakaṭaka, near ŚrīParvata in South India. The *stūpa* became dilated till it assumed the proportions of the universe. The king of Śambhala, Sucandra, wrote down the revelation, went back to his native country of Śambhala, and built a *stūpa* in honour of the Kālacakra. The Tibetan tradition places Śambhala near the Sītā River, that is, the Syr River in Central Asia. Many generations of Kulika kings ruled wisely and handed down the teachings of the Kālacakra. Their power was weakened by raids of *mlecchas* (foreigners) coming from Me-kha (Mecca), that is, Muslim invaders.

Reflecting a time-bound historic event, Kālacakra was affiliated to Akṣobhya, the Great Indeterminate. He is in an embrace with his consort Viśvamātā—the Universal Mother. He dances on the bodies of Anaṅga and Rati, Rudra and Gaurī. As their last creation, Tantric masters express

Kālacakra

The cross-cultural diffusion of the Kālacakra by the 14th Dalai Lama has been effected by conducting initiation rites over the past decades across Asia, USA, Europe and Russia. He has made it a symbol of Tibetan Buddhism. His Holiness performs it every year so that its empowerment leads to birth in the paradise of Śambhala, made famous as the Shangrila. It is the last *tantra,* taught by the Buddha as the *Dharma-kāya* to Sucandra, the king of the Śambhala Empire located in Central Asia. It was revealed at the Dhānyakaṭaka Stūpa in South India. The Drepung Monastery of Lhasa is named after it (dre *'dhānya'* + pung '*kaṭaka*'). The Kālacakra was preserved by the six successors of Sucandra. The sixth of them, Yaśas, had the title Kulika—one who unified all the variant sections of society. The *tantra* prophesies that there will be twenty-five Kulika Kings of Śambhala and the last of them, King Rudracakrin will defeat the barbarian forces and initiate a new golden age. The Kālacakra was introduced into Tibet in 1027 and is the basis of the Tibetan calendar. Its transmission passed through Bu-ston (1290-1364) to Tsoṅ-kha-pa, and its practice is widespread till today. The *tantra* has three parts. The 'outer' part describes the physical world, its arising and geography. The emphasis is on astronomy, time-reckoning and mathematics. The 'inner' part describes the psychological world, like the function of the *nāḍī*s. The 'third' part is devoted to the visualisation *(sādhana)* of the deities in the *maṇḍala.* It has a series of meditation practices, like the technique of inner heat, gtum-mo, (Sanskrit: *caṇḍī*). The practice of *caṇḍī* has been studied by modern science as an aid to survive in extreme cold.

ABOVE: *A monogram of ten letters* H K Ṣ M L V R Y A Ṁ, *called* dásākāro vaśī *in the* Nāma-saṅgīti. *It represents Vairocana who is tenfold. The restraining of the ten winds is* samādhi.

ABOVE AND FACING PAGE: *Kālacakra in union with his consort Viśvamātā. Surrounded by a flaming halo which gleams red and orange all around them, he performs his mystic dance. He is the final creation of Tantric masters in the 10th century to express the wealth of their inner vision, through a new symbol.*

through the instruments in the hands of Kālacakra the inexhaustible wealth of their inner experiences.

The *Kālacakra maṇḍala* has three enclosures which represent the spiritual *(citta),* the verbal *(vāk)* and the physical *(kāya)* planes with its staggering number of 722 deities. All have four separate and elaborate portals of their own. The centre is occupied by Kālacakra embraced by his consort. In the concentric square surrounding it are eight goddesses in the four directions and four intermediate points. In its second encircling square are four Tathāgatas with their consorts. In the next square are the four gateways occupied by eight Bodhisattvas in union with their consorts. The corners have four goddesses accompanied by their male counterparts. The gates are occupied by four angry deities in union with their consorts.

The consort Viśvamātā wears a crown, which is of the nature of Vajrasattva. She is adorned with five types of ornaments, whereas Kālacakra himself has six types of ornaments. The missing type of ornaments on the consort symbolise the white bodhicitta. The sexual union of the deity and consort symbolises the union of method and wisdom. Kālacakra symbolises method *(upāya)* which refers to great bliss. The consort symbolises wisdom *(prajñā),* the realisation of emptiness. Theirs is the union of great bliss and wisdom, realising emptiness. Without the wisdom of indivisible bliss and emptiness, it is impossible to reach the state of full Enlightenment. It is for this reason that Kālacakra symbolising method, and the consort symbolising wisdom, are in intimate union.

The Kālacakra initiation makes manifest the fundamental innate mind of clear light, latent in all experience. In the Kālacakra rites, one performs the withdrawal of all appearances that melt:

> Into light and dissolve into myself.
> I also melt into light and then from within
> The emptiness of unapprehendability
> Again transforms into the aspect of Kālacakra.

Śambhala, the Mythical Land of Kālacakra

At the request of King Sucandra, an emanation of Vajrapāṇi, Śākyamuni Buddha set forth the *Kālacakra Tantra,* on the fifteenth day of the third month. King Sucandra had come from Śambhala (pgs. 115. 116), which Tibetan tradition places to the north of Sītā (Syr) River in Central Asia, surrounded by snow-capped mountains. The King went back to Śambhala, compiled the *tantra* in 12,000 stanzas, wrote a long exposition, and propagated the system. The New Age of Fruition, the Golden Age of Śambhala, will dawn, and generate the impulse toward Enlightenment in the mind stream

FACING PAGE: *Śambhala the legendary kingdom governed by the wise and compassionate Kulika Kings shines as a model society. Their palace of Kalāpa ran into many miles. In the middle of its beautiful park was a temple to Kālacakra built by King Sucandra. The Kulika Kings watch over human affairs and will return to save humanity from the forces of darkness.*

of every sentient being. The great warriors are those whose minds overflow with generosity and compassion.

James Hilton's famous novel, *Lost Horizons,* which was published in 1933, popularised the legend of Śambhala in the English-speaking world, as the Shangrila. It had already exercised a deep influence on the Russian mind since the beginning of the 19th century.

In the centre of the Śambhala country lay the royal palace of Kalāpa. To its south was the architectural *maṇḍala* of Kālacakra built by King Sucandra. King Sucandra was the first of the seven *Dharma* Kings of Śambhala. He was succeeded by a line of twenty-five Kulika kings, each of them credited with a reign of a hundred years. They handed down the sacred teachings of the Kālacakra until they were threatened by the raids of Kla-klo from Me-kha. It is believed that the twenty-fifth and last Kulika king, Rudracakrin, would defeat them and restore *Dharma.* Initiation into the Kālacakra is not only to maintain the practice of its meditation, but also to be ready when the great war of Rudracakrin comes, and when the barbarians will be finally defeated. The Kālacakra is practised as the most developed system 'for transforming mind and body into purity,' in the words of His Holiness the Dalai Lama XIV.

The Kālacakra emphasizes the fourth initiation into a union of supreme immutable bliss and totally supreme emptiness. It is both empiricism and transcendence. The close connection of the Kālacakra and the Gelukpas is underlined by the name of the Drepung Monastery, a translation of Dhānyakaṭaka on whose model it was founded in AD 1419.

King Sucandra as an emanation of Vajrapāṇi, is blue in colour, embraces a consort like himself, wears precious adornments and clothes of divine substance captivating the mind, and through whose kindness great bliss itself dawns in an instant. He sits on a throne held aloft by the Four-faced Brahmā of yellow complexion and Indra of white complexion with a thousand eyes all over his body.

Firm on the rock sits the Kulika king Mahābala, besides his charming consort. He tames all false leaders by means of the sound of the *mantra.* He holds the branch of a tree in the right hand and a flaming wish-granting jewel atop a *Dharmacakra* in the other.

Anantajaya is the twenty-fourth Kulika king. He holds a baton topped by a crossed *vajra* and a chopper in the right hand, and a noose in the left. He is accompanied by his *yoginī.* He precedes King Rudracakrin followed by his two sons, making up thirty-five kings (8 *Dharmarājas* + 25 Kulika kings + 2 sons). A lake can be seen in some scrolls,

FACING PAGE: *In the legendary kingdom of Śambhala of the Kulika Kings, Kālacakra flourished. It is said that the golden age of Śambhala will dawn one day to generate the impulse towards Enlightenment.*

perhaps an allusion to the Altaic word '*gol*' meaning 'river'. The Kulika kings came from a kingdom by the Sita River .

The scintillating colours of the scrolls connected with Kālacakra remind one of human intelligence attuned to experiencing the brilliance of the bright blue sky. Blue is the colour of *dhyāna* or meditation. The beauty of trees and mountains is an ideal setting for a hierophant to meditate, so that the Śambhala vision tunes him to awaken in the realm of the cosmic mirror, where there is no beginning and no end—it is a state of vastness, of immensity, and immensity is Being. The Kulika king Anantajaya is the Ultimate *(ananta)* Victor *(jaya)* and represents the possibility to give birth to the universal monarch within oneself, when one has completely identified oneself with the lineage of the wisdom of the Kulika kings. The mountains are the solid, and represent completely stable Truth which never wavers.

Two-Armed Heruka

Heruka (right) is in the centre, multiplied as four manifestations at the bottom. In the four corners are the four dancing *ḍākinīs.*

The ninefold *maṇḍala* of the Supreme Heruka (Tibetan: Che-mchog-dpal-dgu) are the Eight Vibrations of Practice out of which arise the Hundred Wrathful and Peaceful deities. The hierophant's practice is to discover the external, internal and secret characteristics of the divinities by visualisation of their form, recitation of their *mantra,* and meditation reifying their symbolic qualities. The Supreme Heruka in his wrathful form is the *Yidam* or tutelary deity of the meditator, and the four *ḍākinīs* are movements of the Void, the matrix of awareness. Heruka is blue, carries a *vajra* in the right hand and the left embraces the consort and does not have the cranium *(kapāla)* in the central figure. The four emanations do have the cranium. His necklace is a chain of half-a-hundred severed heads. His head has five skulls.

In the Nyingmapa doctrine, there is a state of absolute voidness, uncreated, without beginning, in which there are neither Buddhas nor beings who might strive to Buddhahood. This state is the quintessential body. In it the various modes of being flow together. Thus it transcends both the *samsaric* and *nirvanic* states.

Six-Armed Saṁvara

Six-armed Saṁvara (p. 123) embraces his consort Vajravārāhī whose colour is red like the pomegranate flower. With a *vajra* she threatens evil-doers, and is mantled by the romance of her thrilled body. Saṁvara appears terrible, clad in garments of tiger-skin and elephant-skin, with a garland of fifty human

FACING PAGE: *The divine body of Heruka and his consort represent the absolute unification of all duality which is the ultimate principle of union or Joy Innate.*

Yab-Yum

Yab-Yum means 'Father and Mother' or male and female consorts, represented in Tibetan icons in sexual union. They symbolise the unity of the masculine and feminine principles. The male represents compassion *(karuṇā)* and skillful means *(upāya-kauśalya),* and the female consort is linked to transcendental wisdom *(prajñā).* The symbol of universal creation is transposed into sexual union. Wisdom and skillful means, or void and compassion melt into unity in the *bodhicitta.* The two components are an invitation to reintegrate the duality of phenomenal experience into the plane of the Absolute or *bodhicitta* from which we have decayed. Instead of repressing the inborn libido of creatures, it is well to transfer it to higher planes. The *Atiyoga* texts explain the *Yab* as the means and the *māyā*-body, while the *Yum* is wisdom or transcendental consciousness. The *māyā*-body and transcendental consciousness are the reintegration flowing together on the plane of ultimate reality. The 'great voidness' corresponds to great pleasure *(mahāsukha).* It is entry into the consciousness of Being, beyond any qualification. Tsoṅ-kha-pa says that the *Yab* is the enlightened attitude which is the specific cause of Buddhahood. The *Yum* is the discriminative acumen, which immediately intuits that *Śūnyatā* is the cause of bringing into the world four sons, that are the four philosophical schools of the Vaibhāṣikas, Sautrāntikas, Vijñānavādins and Mādhyamikas. Just as both the father and the mother are necessary to produce a child, likewise both an enlightened attitude and discriminative acumen are necessary for the arising of Buddhahood.

Yab	*Yum*
means *(upāya)*	wisdom *(prajñā)*
rāga	void *(śūnyatā)*
māyā-body	transcendental consciousness
enlightened attitude	discriminative acumen

skulls. He tramples on the prostrate Kālarātrī and Bhairava. He displays the nine dramatic sentiments.

In the two principal hands he holds the *vajra* and *vajra*-marked bell. These are the hands that embrace the consort. The other right hands hold the chopper *(kartrī)* and skull-drum *(ḍamaru)* and the left hands have the vajra-noose *(vajra-pāśa)* and the cranium *(kapāla)*. The vajra and bell in the original hands symbolise that he is the union of illumination and compassion, the *bodhicitta* of insubstantiality

ABOVE: *Hayagrīva has three horses' heads in his crown. The horse symbolises the trampling of evil. Hayagrīva is invoked to destroy the enemy. He is also the protector of horses. He has three heads: the blue head signifies heroic energy; the white head symbolises the mind of pure white faith, and the head of the morning colour signifies great compassion.*

and compassion, and the embrace unites the means *(upāya)* and transcendental wisdom *(prajñā)*. The chopper severs pride and destroys the sins of the world-system. The skull-drum proclaims joyous tidings. The noose is the knowledge that holds the nature of sentient beings. The cranium-bowl does away with all ideas of substance and non-substance and is the symbol of supreme beatitude. The *khaṭvāṅga* (skull-staff) is marked with the *vajra*-symbol of illumination.

Vajravārāhī's body is red as she is dedicated to the good of creatures. She has only one face to indicate the essential sameness of all things; and two hands: because truth is two-fold, absolute and relative. She is marked with six auspicious symbols, is nude and the embodiment of innate *(sahaja)* pleasure. She is nude with dishevelled hair because she has been set free from the illusions that hide the essence of things.

Twelve-Armed Saṁvara

He (p. 124) embraces his consort Vajravārāhi representing the impersonality of passion. Away from the simple serenity of Śākyamuni, and the candour of his message, in Saṁvara, we are face-to-face with the metaphysical daring of the bejewelled *sambhoga-kāya*—'enjoyment body'—passionately embracing his transcendant consort. Here is serenity identified with passion, crystalline Enlightenment with the fire of love, yet all beyond the metaphysical filigree into the eternal depths of the experience of the futile and fleeting character of what we call the world. He stands in the *ālīḍha* posture of outstretched legs on the prostrate forms of Bhairava and Kālarātrī. He is blue in colour. His four faces on the east, south, west and north are blue, green, red and yellow, respectively. He is twelve-armed. With the two principal arms carrying the *vajra* and the *vajra*-marked bell, he embraces his consort Vajravārāhī. With the second pair he carries the elephant-skin from which blood is trickling down. In the remaining four right hands he holds the skull drum or *ḍamaru,* the axe, the knife and the trident. The four left hands show the *vajra*-marked skull-staff or *khaṭvāṅga,* the cranium-cup full of blood, the *vajra*-noose and the severed head of Brahmā. He displays in full the nine dramatic sentiments. His twelve hands are the collective purity in the interpretation of the twelve-fold causal concatenation.

Sixteen-Armed Hevajra

The famous *Hevajra Tantra* is devoted to him. He towers in the centre, with eight heads and sixteen arms. In this form he is known as the Cranium-bearing *(Kapāladhara)* Hevajra (p. 125). This is

FACING PAGE: *Six-armed Saṁvara with his consort Vajravārāhī.*

to distinguish him from the other sixteen-armed Śastradhara Hevajra who carries weapons *(śastra)* and other attributes. In each of the sixteen hands he carries as many cranial cups in which are found animals on the right and deities on the left.

The original hands clasp his consort, the blue Nairātmā, who holds a cranium in the right hand and a chopper in the left.

The main face of Hevajra is black, those on the right are successively white, black and black, those on the left are red, black and black. The face on top is the colour of smoke or of the colour of a bee. With his four legs he crushes the four Māras.

Hevajra is one of the principal tutelary deities *(Yidam)* of the Sakyapa denomination. Hevajra may be counted as the second wave in the development of texts and monastic institutions that laid the foundation of the Buddhist teachings of the Second Transmission. The Sakyapa lineages commence with the translator Ḥbrog-mi (AD 992–1072), from the noble Khon family of the Tsang province. After the foundation of the Sakya Monastery in the Sakya Valley in AD 1073, numerous monks began translating and studying books, contemplating and practising advanced tantric techniques of the Path and Fruition teachings, which were derived by the great Siddha Virūpa from the *Hevajra Tantra.* In the magic aura of visions, gods and goddesses are born out of ritual objects,

ABOVE: *Twelve-armed Saṁvara from the* Abhidhānottara Tantra. *He crushes the head of Kāla Bhairava with his right leg and tramples on the Red Kālī with the left one.*

as acts of cult get a name. The invocation *He-vajra* —O Vajra!— became the hypostasis of the Akṣobhya family and expresses his omnipotence by the multiplication of heads, arms and feet, and he becomes the divine means of beatific vision. Hevajra is the realisation of the essential identity of *nirvāṇa* and *saṁsāra; he* means compassion and *vajra* means wisdom, symbolising the Supreme. He

ABOVE: *Sixteen-armed Hevajra with eight faces and four feet. He is the main deity of the* Hevajra Tantra, 2.5.5, *where he tells his consort: 'The Joy Innate I am in essence, and impassioned with great passion... . My inner nature is tranquil. Holding Nairātmyā in loving embrace, I am possessed of tranquil bliss.'*

is consubstantiated with Nairātmā or the 'absence of the notion of self.' The dominating concept of two-in-one (zungjuk), indicates the identity of wisdom and compassion, the pure essence of knowledge where all differences between *saṁsāra* and *nirvāṇa* cease.

Vajrakīla

Above is an illustrated manuscript on the rites of Vajrakīla (Tibetan: Rdo-rje-phur-pa, or Rdo-rje-phur-bu), a deification of the magic dagger to nail down harmful and hostile forces. Vajrakīla is one of the most powerful of *Dharmapāla*s whose potent exorcist rites have been equally performed from the Nyingmapas to the Sakyapas, down to the Gelukpas. He is a terrific aspect of Heruka. On his back are adamantine wings. He is represented with three faces: the one on the right is white, the central one blue and that on the left is red. He has six hands: the two right hands grasp the nine-pronged and five-pronged *vajras;* the upper left hand is in the threatening *tarjānī-mudrā* and the lower one brandishes a trident. The two 'original' hands tightly hold the *phur-bu* dagger and at the same time embrace the consort. A tiger-skin constitutes his loin cloth. The two legs weigh down on Rudra and Rudrāṇī.

His consort is Ḥkhor-lo-rgyas-ḥdebs-ma, blue in body, with a *vajra*-bell in her right hand, while with her left she offers her mate a skull-cup brimming over with blood.

Exoteric Dharmarāja

He is Chos-rgyal phyi-sgrub in Tibetan, has the face of a buffalo and also rides a buffalo. In his right hand he brandishes a club with a skull, and in the

ABOVE: *Rituals to Vajrakīla are performed for genuine altruistic motives and not for personal benefit. They are performed to stop evil, for the welfare of dharma, and for the welfare of the state. Vajrakīla's animating energy effects the destruction of enemies and prevents rain. Among the Nyingmapas he is the principal* yidam *or tutelary deity of the sect and is an aspect of Heruka.*

left holds a noose in the *tarjanī-mudrā*. His three eyes blaze like the apocalyptic fires. His hair rises in flames. He wears a garland of severed heads. The Wheel of *Dharma* on his breast shows that Tsoṅ-kha-pa, who founded the Gelukpa denomination, appointed him in a grand ceremony as the protector of the Gelukpas. On his left is Camuṇḍā in pale blue, while Yama is dark blue. Camuṇḍā holds a cranium cup in her right hand and a trident in her left. Her breasts are emaciated and her hair hang loose. Her dress is of ox-skin and black silks according to the *Rin-ḥbyuṅ*. Both are on a buffalo, under which is a woman. Their bodies are moved by inner fierceness. Death, the Daughter of Darkness and the Sister of Sleep as the eternal somnia, is the source of life, and not only of spiritual life, but of the resurrection of matter as well. It is a transformation of form without annihilating the essence. It symbolises dematerialisation as well as the progress of evolution. Continual death and decomposition is infused with an all-pervading luxuriance and magnificence of life. A tree falls and rots, thousands of plants invest, assault and prosper in turn. Life thrives on death. *Dharmarāja* is the cycle of living that gives nourishment to the vortex of new lives. *Dharma* is upholding (the root *dhar* means 'to hold, 'sustain') the dense tissue of vitality and *Dharmarāja* is the invisible time that glides on in the cycle of life!

Six-Armed Mahākāla

Six-armed Mahākāla (Tibetan: Mgon-po-phyag-drug) is dark blue in colour, one-faced, three-eyed, has hair ablaze like fire with a tuft tied with a wriggling serpent, has a crown of skulls and a garland of severed heads, wears a tiger skin and tramples on the elephant-headed white Gaṇapati. His six hands hold a rosary of human skulls, skull drum *(ḍamaru)* and chopper in front of the breast; the left hands have a trident with a skull and heart transfixed (*śūla* according to the *Sādhanamālā*), snare with two vajras attached to its end *(vajrapāśa),* and the blood-filled skull-bowl *(kapāla)* in front of the breast. His body is covered with numerous ornaments: bangles of bells are on his hands and feet; he wears a green necklace, red earrings, ornaments of human bone, a crown of five human skulls, and a garland of freshly severed human heads; the whole figure is surrounded by fiercely blazing flames. As such he is the 'Universal Protector', that is, the main guardian deity of the Gelukpa and Sakyapa and occupies a prominent place in the Nyingmapa and Kadampa Schools as well.

Kṣetrapāla

Kṣetrapāla (Tibetan: Zhiṅ-skyoṅ; p. 128) is the foremost of the four *yakṣa* ministers of the Six-

armed Mahākāla. His right hand shakes the chopper (gri-gug) to terrify both gods and demons. The left hand holds a skull-cup full of blood. His *bali-vidhi* by the monk Tikṣanti, describes him as follows: On top of a sun-*maṇḍala* comes forth—from the syllable *'kṣe'*—Kṣetrapāla of a dark-blue colour, with one face and two hands. Lifting with his right hand a chopper skyward, he cuts with it the life-roots of enemies and obstacle-creating demons; his left hand holds a skull-cup, filled with a heart-blood of enemies and *vighnas*. His mouth is wide open and he bares his four sharp teeth, causing enemies to wail aloud. Rolling his three bloodshot eyes, he stares full of hatred at the enemies and obstacle-creating demons. His eyebrows and the hair of his face are of a flaming yellow-red hue; the hair of his head is yellow-brown and it stands on end. He wears a dry human skull as head-ornament, a human skin covers the upper portion of his body, and a tiger-skin serves as a loin-cloth. He has an ugly and terrifying body. Riding a black wild bear, he resides in the centre of a vehemently blazing fire.

Pañjara-Mahākāla

Pañjara-Mahākāla (Tibetan: Gur Mgon; p. 131) or the Mahākāla from the *Pañjara Tantra* is the main deity of the Sakyapas. His omnipotence is invoked against powers of evil. He is a symbol of the fierce power of Akṣobhya who reduces to dust demons and forces adverse to *Dharma*. He is the Great Mahākāla (Mgon-chen) with one ferocious face, in contradistinction to the Junior Mahākāla (Mgon-chuṅ) with four faces. He is represented by a dark blue body, one face, three eyes, two hands, hair standing on end and a diadem of five human heads. In the right hand he clasps the *vajra-katarī* (crooked knife with a hilt of the form of a *vajra*); while the left hand holds a skull-cup filled with the blood of demons he has annihilated. Between his two hands, he holds the miraculous *gaṇḍī* at breast level. His distinctive symbol is the *gaṇḍī,* a piece of wood used for striking the hours in monasteries. It is a terrifying club which punishes everyone offending the sanctity of the word. He watches over the fulfilment of vows and promises, and thereby guarantees faith. The supreme vow is pursuing Enlightenment. If a person does not fulfil this vow, he will be devoured by the dark world of instincts that pull him away from redeeming light. His loin-cloth is made of tiger-skin. His ornaments are the eight serpents. He wears a garland of just beheaded fifty blood-dripping human heads. He is accompanied by blue *garuḍas*, blackbirds, black dogs and jackals: all symbols of death.

Guardian of the Buddhist *Dharma,* he reigns over good and evil, cuts the life-thread of those

FACING PAGE: *Kṣetrapāla resides in the Śītavana Cemetery near Bodhgaya. The cemetery, as terrifying as his body, is full of the howling of witches, the splashing of blood and the blaring of thighbone trumpets. He reduces all kinds of evil powers to dust, and cuts the life-thread of his enemies.*

who act contrary to the commands of the guru. The richness of forms in the retinue of the main deity is a reflection of the complex elements of varied origin, age and content, continuing from prehistoric traditions to more recent influences. The folk heritage of both India and Tibet influences the spiritual life of Tibet. The immense world of the demonic and the divine, the marvellous happenings and epic deeds defend against obstacles and dangers. The presiding deity stands by the side of the faithful in their incessant struggle against secret adversaries. They ensure the formation of a new world, consecrated according to the scriptures.

Guhyasamāja Akṣobhyavajra

In the Guhyasamāja system there can be a number of central deities of the *maṇḍala*. The prime deity is Akṣobhyavajra, and Mañjuvajra is the second central deity of importance with his independent *maṇḍala*.

Guhyasamāja Akṣobhyavajra (p. 132), with his consort Ādiprajñā— Primordial Wisdom—is seated in the *vajra* posture, is dark blue in colour, distinct from the light blue complexion of his consort, has three faces which are white, dark blue and red, and six arms. The original hands are crossed against the breast and hold a *vajra* and bell which express phenomental polarities. They are in the *vajra-hūṁkāra mudrā,* and at the same time hold the consort *(prajñā)* in tight embrace. The upper right and left hands hold a *cakra* (wheel) and jewel *(maṇi).* The two lower hands hold a lotus and sword of wisdom *(prajñā-khaḍga).* The *vajra-hūṁkāra-mudrā* symbolises steadfast, unshakeable exertion. The Gurla Mandhata in Western Tibet is considered to be his paradise.

The consort Ādiprajñā is consubstantiated with Akṣobhyavajra, who she encircles, and possesses the same attributes. She has three faces: red, light blue and white. Her original hands embrace the *Yab* at the back, the upper hands hold the jewel and wheel, while the lower ones carry the sword of wisdom and a white lotus.

Guhyasamāja is the most ancient and fundamental *tantra* of Vajrayāna. The psychic process of realisation according to the *Guhyasamāja Tantra* 'makes it clear that when the *bodhicitta* or the Will to Enlightenment mingles with *śūnya* or the Infinite Spirit in the highest state of meditation the mind-sky is filled with innumerable visions and scenes until at last, like sparks the individuals visualize letters or germ syllables, which gradually assume the shape of deities, first indistinct, then changing into perfect, glorious and living forms, the embodiment of the infinite *Śūnya.* They appear in bright, effulgent,

FACING PAGE: *The cult of Pañjara Mahākāla was established by the Sakyapas. Today, he is an important* dharmapāla *of the Gelukpas. The* tantric *command staff symbolises dominance over religious enemies.*

gorgeous and divine beauty in form, ornaments and dress.'

Guhyasamāja Mañjuvajra (Gsaṅ-ba-ḥdus-pa Ḥjam-paḥi-rdo-rje)

The *maṇḍala* of Mañjuvajra (p. 135) is the very first *maṇḍala* in the *Niṣpanna-yogāvalī,* an outstanding and most popular work on *maṇḍala*s ever since Abhayākaragupta wrote it eight hundred years ago. The principal deity is Vajrasattva in his emanation as Mañjuvajra, red like vermilion, embracing his consort with the original hands. In the four others, he carries a sword, arrow, lotus and bow. His light is infinite *(anantābha):* all Tathāgatas are luminous elements.

As the prime emanation of Vajradhara, he is in the *sambhoga-kāya,* fully decked with royal ornaments, and enthroned in a grand shrine. He is blue in colour: blue has the chromatic sensitivity that beckons into the farthest regions of spirituality. Blue is active power. His right hand touches the earth in the *bhūmi-sparśa mudrā,* while the left lies opened upwards in the lap. The *bhūmi-sparśa mudrā* alludes to victory over Māra, as Akṣobhya originated as a symbol of the unchangeableness of the Buddha's condition. Once Enlightenment is achieved, it cannot be lost. It transfers the enlightened one to a spiritual plane which is the kingdom of the Absolute. His mount is the elephant, two of which support his throne. He sits in the adamantine seat of *vajra-paryaṅka* and represents the element of consciousness *(vijñāna).*

The projection of the Supreme Vajradhara into the manifold is his operation in the world, his descent in the mind of the meditator, the assimilation of the macro cosmos with the micro cosmos *(dehe viśvasya mānanam),* the emanation of the universe in the body. As meditation reaches a higher stage, the *maṇḍala* is our body itself.

The *Guhyasamāja* derives its philosophical background from the Mādhyamika philosophy. The *maṇḍala* is the luminous universe that is contained in this very body of ours in the sublime stages of meditation.

Lineage of the Jñānapāda School of Guhyasamāja

The Sakyapa School (p. 136) illustrates the lineage of legendary and historical masters of the *Guhyasamāja Tantra* according to the Jñānapāda School. Among historical figures both Indian and Tibetan Sakyapa masters are shown as the transient expression of the eternal *Dharma.* The *Guhyasamāja* is an important *tantra* which had been translated already in the period of Early

FACING PAGE: *Guhyasamāja Akṣobhyavajra is the symbol of purification in the meditative process. He corresponds to the knowledge that lets us see all things as subjective reflection; cannot be swayed by defilement or constructive thought, and is firm without flux.*

Propagation of Buddhism in Tibet by the scholar, Lce Bkra-śis. The Nyingmapa School considers it to be the most important text among the eighteen classes of their *tantras*. In the period of the Later Propagation in the 10th century, the great translator Rin-chen-bzaṅ-po again translated this *tantra,* its commentaries and other related texts, with the help of the Indian master Śraddhākara-varman. The translation of Rin-chen-bzaṅ-po is the canonical version included in the Tibetan Kanjur.

There are two schools of thought regarding the interpretation of the *Guhyasamāja:* (i) the Ārya School, and (ii) the Jñānapāda School (Tibetan: (i) Ḥphags lugs and (ii) Ye-śes-zhabs lugs.)

The Ārya School is headed by the tantric Nāgārjuna who wrote several commentaries of this *tantra.* His *Pañcakrama* or Five Sequences is authoritative for *yoga.* His interpretation uses *yogācāra* vocabulary, and stresses the Three Lights and Clear Light.

The Jñānapāda School is named after Buddhaśri-jñānapāda. He was versed in all branches of Buddhist learning. From Haribhadra in Takṣaśilā he heard about the *Prajñā-pāramitā* and many other treatises. He visited Oḍḍiyāna in search of *tantras*. There he studied many of them with Lalitavajra. He learned the essence from a *yoginī* and practised meditation. He travelled far and wide to several towns to grasp the meaning of Ultimate Essence. He became a *yogin* possessed of pure wisdom. Mañjughoṣa permitted him to compose works for the benefit of future generations. Jñānapāda wrote treatises exemplifying both the stages of evolution and devolution.

Vajrapāṇi

The dark blue Vajrapāṇi (Tibetan: Phyag-na-rdo-rje or Phyag-rdor for short; p. 137) wields the *vajra* in his uplifted right hand. According to a commentary on the *Prajñā-pāramitā,* the *vajra* is the inner symbol of *bodhicitta* and the outer symbol of destruction and suppression of sorrow and vexation. The Chinese traveller Hsüan-tsang mentions his worship in India in the 7th century. He has several manifestations. Alpacaṇḍa Vajrapāṇi emerges from a flaming halo, gnashing his teeth, a snake hung from the neck and shoulders as a scarf; he has a less ferocious aspect, that is, he is *alpa*—less—and *caṇḍa*—fierce.

Vajrapāṇi is the implacable enemy of demons. The reason is explained in the following legend. Once upon a time all the Buddhas met together on the top of Mount Meru to deliberate upon the best means of procuring the Elixir of Life *(amṛta)* which lies concealed at the bottom of the ocean. The demons were in possession of the

FACING PAGE: *Guhyasamāja Mañjuvajra. Within his breast is a gnosis-being* (jñāna-sattva). *At the heart of the gnosis-being is a moon topped by a sword on whose hilt is the sacred syllable* 'MAṂ', *as a symbol of the concentration-being* (dhyāna-sattva).

powerful poison *halāhala,* and were using it to bring destruction on mankind. To procure the antidote, the Buddhas decided to churn the ocean with Mount Meru. When the *amṛta* had risen to the surface of the water, they put it in the keeping of Vajrapāṇi, until they should decide on the best means of using it; but Vajrapāṇi left the Elixir of Life a moment unguarded and the monster, Rāhu, stole it. Then followed a fearful struggle for the possession of the *amṛta.* Rāhu was conquered in the end, but the Elixir of Life had been defiled, and the Buddhas, to punish Vajrapāṇi, forced him to drink it, whereupon he became dark blue from the poison mixed with the *amṛta.*

Yamāntaka

Yamāntaka is blue and naked, has three heads, each with a third eye, and his six hands hold an axe-knife,

ABOVE: *Vajrapāṇi is identical to Indra. He had promised in the presence of Mahābrahmā to protect the* dharma *of the Buddha. In his outer aspect, he destroys the enemies of* dharma *while in his inner aspect, he suppresses evil. He is the energy aspect of the awakened state of mind.*

FACING PAGE: *This* thaṅka *shows the transmission lineage of the eminent masters of the Jñānapāda school of interpreting the* Guhyasamāja Tantra.

a *vajra, cakra,* sword, lotus and a cranium in the main arms embracing the consort.

His eyes and eyebrows flame like the cosmic fire at the end of aeons. He is of a terrifying aspect meant to repel all adverse forces. With the hatchet he removes false imaginings. He drives away maleficent forces, errors and delusions that keep us away from the crystal-clear light of truth. His awe-inspring door-keepers do not grant the agents of ignorance entrance.

Yamāntaka, Exterminator of Death, killed Yama or death, which means the granting of endless life. One who meditates on this archetypal deity conquers his own mortality, his fear of cessation. In the moment of realisation the mind experiences the self as obliterated and that paves the way for Enlightenment. Yamāntaka encodes sensitivities that open up sequences of contemplative unfoldments. Tsoṅ-kha-pa practised visualisation of Red Yamāntaka, to overcome dangers to health and prolong the life span. Yamāntaka is the terrifying form of Mañjuśrī, the embodiment of Absolute Wisdom.

Mañjuśrī went down to the windowless iron fortress of Yama, Lord of Death. To subdue Yama, Mañjuśrī assumed the form of Red Yamāntaka, or Death magnified to infinity. In Yamāntaka, the Terminator *(antaka)* of Death *(Yama),* the deadlines of Death are terminated.

Vajrabhairava

Tibetan exegesis interprets the characteristics of Vajrabhairava as follows: the ascetic topknot, standing up, means that he is consubstantiated with the five mystic gnoses. He has a terrifying aspect because he drives hostile forces *(Māra)* away. His sixteen feet are a symbol of the sixteen kinds of insubstantiality. His nudity is meant to express that all things are without birth. The erect member means that he is consubstantiated with eternal bliss. The thirty-four arms are a symbol of the thirty-four coefficients of Enlightenment. The knife is there because he slays ignorance, the javelin because he analyses what is falsely imagined concerning the subject and its object, the pestle means the concentration of awareness, the razor because he slays sin, the goad indicates the submission of the body and the word, the axe because he cuts off the mind's error, the spear because he annihilates false theories, the arrow because he pierces false imaginings, the hook because he drags (towards salvation), the club because he breaks down the veil derived from *karma,* the *khaṭvāṅga* (skull-staff) because his nature is consubtantiated with the thought of Enlightenment, the disc because he sets the Wheel of *Dharma* in motion, the *vajra* because he is consubstantiated with the fifth gnosis, the hammer because he cleaves covetousness

FACING PAGE: *Vajrabhairava with the face of a buffalo, 34 arms and 16 feet repels all adverse forces. He drives away all delusions that keep us from the crystal clear light of Truth.*

asunder, the sword because he bestows various magical powers like those belonging to the sword, among others, the drumlet because through the supreme bliss so symbolised, he admonishes all the Tathāgatas, the skull full of blood because he stimulates us to observe vows, Brahmā's head accomplishes the good of created beings through his compassion, the shield because he triumphs over the works of all Māras, the foot because he bestows on those who meditate the same rank as the Buddhas, the noose because he takes possession of (literally ties) Supreme Wisdom, the bow because he triumphs over the three worlds, bowels because he helps us to understand the insubstantiality of things, the bell to represent consubstantiality with supreme gnosis, the hand because he is capable of doing all things, the rag picked up in cemeteries because he destroys the veil of ignorance which prevents us from recognising that all things lack an essence of their own, an impaled man because he penetrates deep into the conception that all things lack substance, the (triangular) fireplace symbolises germinal light, the freshly-cut head because he is full of the ambrosia of compassion, the hand in a threatening posture because he terrifies fiends, the three-pointed spear symbolises the conception that spirit, word and body have only one essence, a fluttering piece of cloth because all things are *māyā*. The beings he tramples underfoot

ABOVE: *Vajrabhairava is one of the most venerated deities in the Gelukpa denomination. He fights evil and redeems beings from forces adverse to* Dharma. *His eyelashes and eyelids, beard and body-hair are all aflame like the cosmic fire at the end of aeons.*

symbolise the mystic powers derived from him. The terrific manifestations are integral for expelling and suppressing the forces adverse to goodness, to *Dharma*.

In powerful delineation and vibrant colours is Vajrabhairava, with nine faces, thirty-four arms and sixteen feet. He is one of the most venerated deities, especially among the Gelukpas and Sakyapas. He is the sacred terror so that the crowds never betray the precepts of Śākyamuni. He is the tremendum that dominates the efficacy of spiritual achievement. He is the fusion of two aspects: the blessed aspect and the irate aspect (zhi-khro): the emanation of the double aspect of Mañjuśrī. He is so fierce as to destroy all forces contrary to *Dharma*. He suppresses all evil that derives from malefic forces. Vajrabhairava is thus a god of redemption, one who fights against evil and triumphs. The left legs are stretched, the right ones are folded. He is able to swallow the triple world. He guffaws loudly, has the tongue rolled, gnaws his teeth and his eyebrows raised in a frown

The eyes and the eyelashes flame like the cosmic fire at the time of destruction of the universe. His hair is yellow and erect. His eyelashes and eyelids, beard and body-hair—all are aflame like the cosmic fire at the end of aeons. The central face is that of a buffalo, it expresses profound rage and has horns. The terrific manifestations are integral

ABOVE: *Vajrabhairava adorned with ornaments of the charnel ground. The frightful gnosis-king, smoke-coloured, darkness-destroyer, the angry slayer of Yama, he stands amidst a blazing mass of fire.*

for expelling and suppressing the forces adverse to goodness, to *Dharma.* He signifies that *Dharma* protects, if it is protected.

Vajradhara

Vajradhara (facing page) is dressed in royal attire, with diadem, necklaces, earrings, armlets, bracelets and anklets. The figure is deep blue, with hands crossed over the chest, with the *vajra* in the right and the bell in the left. He is the supreme guru of the Kargyupa, and the principal deity of this sect whose origins go back to Marpa. Marpa was a disciple of Naropa and the master of the supreme *yogin* and poet Milarepa.

Vajradhara occupies a prominent position in the mystical experience of the Gelukpas too. The mystic identifies himself with Vajradhara, who becomes embodied in the Five Tathāgatas as soon as he begins to project himself in the world of contingency. As the symbol of cosmic consciousness, he is the favourite deity of the ascetics.

Vajradhara is the spotless brightness, the prime emanation of the lively inner experience of the truth, and the unfailingness of this state as the very name indicates. He is the Absolute, beyond the Five Buddhas, transcending them and nevertheless permeating them as the source of all apparent phenomena.

Vajrasattva

Vajrasattva, the Adamantime Being (Tibetan: Rdo-rje-sems-dpaḥ; p. 145), is the first principle, incorruptible like the *vajra,* not subject to decay, and transcending the Five Tathāgatas. He is white, seated on a lotus, holds the *vajra* in the right hand with the palm upwards and the *vajra*-marked bell in his left hand resting on the left thigh. He is two-armed and one-faced.

Vajrasattva is the visible symbol of cosmic consciousness in its absolute and incorruptible essence. He is the unsubstantiality of things itself, the being who is of himself—*svayambhū-rūpa.* He is above the pentad because he is undifferentiated and, in the schools of *Anuttara Yoga,* the sixth Buddha. He is always represented with a bell and a *vajra.* These instruments, essential to every esoteric Buddhist liturgy, are symbols: the first of the emptiness of all things and of the awareness of such emptiness, the second of the meditative process, which translates in psychological experiences and spiritual realisations. So when Vajrasattva is represented embracing his consort, the same symbolism is expressed by human figures: god is *vajra,* the consort is the bell, that is, the synthesis of the two elements from which Supreme Enlightenment is derived: gnosis and compassion.

FACING PAGE: *An appliqué* thaṅka *of Vajradhara of deep blue colour, representing the interior illumination which is by nature luminous like the azure blue sky. The bell symbolises wisdom and* vajra *denotes compassion, the two fundamental co-efficients from which the spark of Supreme Truth will shine forth.*

Māyājāla-Mañjuvajra

The *Niṣpanna-yogāvalī* is a manual of *maṇḍalas* by Abhayākaragupta who lived in the last quarter of the 11th century. This manual describes in detail two *maṇḍalas* of the two forms of Mañjuvajra. The first Mañjuvajra is in the system of the Guhyasamāja and the second Mañjuvajra is in the system of the *Māyājāla Tantra*.

Mañjuvajra of the *Māyājāla* (left) as the sovereign of the *maṇḍala* sits in the noble attitude on a moon, over a blossomed lotus supported by a lion. He radiates the charm of glowing gold. His consort is Vajradhātvīśvarī, irradiated from his own being. She is white in complexion, and shares the throne with her lord. Mañjuvajra has three faces and six arms. His body complexion is red like vermilion, and likewise the central face. The right face is blue and the left is white. His six hands hold the following attributes listed below:

Right hands:
Sword;
Arrow;
Varada mudrā

Left hands:
Blue lotus;
Manuscript of the *Prajñā-pāramitā;*
Bow

ABOVE: Maṇḍala *of Māyājāla-Mañjuvajra.*

The Bardo Maṇḍala

The *maṇḍala* of Bardo Thos-grol portrays the nature of the mind in its beautiful or terrible, peaceful or wrathful projections. The projections are as they appear when the consciousness is no longer grounded in a physical body. Recognition of the essential reality of the seductive and terrifying forms leads to Enlightenment. Traditionally ascribed to Padmasambhava, this centuries-old scripture is read aloud to the dying to help them attain liberation.

In the centre is Guru Padmasambhava, with a *vajra* in his right hand and a skull-cup in the left, and a *khakkhara* staff in the crook of his right arm. Padmasambhava is the first of his eight manifestations as Saroruhavajra.

The *vajra* is symbolic of mastery over life and the skull filled with blood symbolises renunciation of life. On top is Avalokiteśvara and above him is Samantabhadra as Ādibuddha in the *Yab-Yum*. Padmasambhava is flanked by his two consorts, Ye-śes-mtsho-rgyal and Mandāravā. King Khri Sroṅ-lde-btsan who invited him to Tibet on the suggestion of Bodhisattva Śāntarakṣita are both seated below his lotus-seat. His palace is guarded by the four *Lokapālas* who can be seen at the four gates of the four directions. The spirituality of the magical and the mysterious radiates the beauty and the blessings of the Guru.

ABOVE: *Vajrasattva cleanses all defilements, sins and obscurations, grants all realisations, and makes the mind glorious. At his heart is the gnosis-being* (jñāna-sattva). *He epitomises the play of gnosis and great bliss. He is above The Five Transcendental Buddhas because he precedes any evolution into the multiple. His bell and* vajra *symbolise the emptiness of all things and the meditative process to translate them into spiritual realisation.*

Bon

Bon enshrines the pre-Buddhist beliefs, practices and rites of Tibet saturated with Buddhist elements. As there was no writing before the introduction of Buddhism, we can only surmise that proto-Bon had beliefs on after-life, animal sacrifices, royal consecration and funerary rites. Bon, as it is practised today, is heavily influenced by Buddhist forms and doctrines, though the indigenous cosmology, sacred narratives and pantheon form the core of Bon. The basic teachings of Bon are virtually identical with Buddhism. An enlightened being in Bon is saṅs-rgyas or the Buddha, and Enlightenment is byaṅ-chub or Bodhi. The word 'chos' *(Dharma)* is replaced by 'bon' in Bon: thus 'chos-sku' (*Dharma*-body) is 'bon-sku'—'bon body'. Like Buddhism, the Bonpo Canon is divided into *Kanjur* and *Tanjur*. The *Kanjur* has scriptures of revealed words of Gshen-rab, the founder of Bon. Gshen-chen Klu-dgaḥ (996-1035) discovered the Bon scriptures around 1017 and they are a substantial part of the Canon. In 1405, Śes.rab.rgyal.mtshan (1356-1415) founded the Menri Monastery, the most important Bon centre till today. A special role was played by the western region of Tibet, the Shangshung Kingdom, in the development of its doctrinal system. In pre-Buddhist Tibet, the kings were protected by the bonpos who were responsible for the exorcism of hostile forces. In transformed Bon, elements of the folk religion and Buddhist doctrines were fused under Gshen-rab, the founder of the Bon School.

The *maṇḍala* of Bardo comprises 110 deities. They dawn to the deceased for fourteen of the forty-nine days of the Bardo existence. During the first seven days dawn the peaceful deities, while wrathful deities dawn for the next seven days. As one recovers from a swoon one thinks: 'What has happened?' One has to recognise this as the intermediate existence of Bardo. The phenomenal appearances are radiances and deities. The whole of heaven appears deep blue. As such the background of the *thaṅka* is deep blue. The Five Tathāgatas who appear from the first to the fifth day are shown on top. All of them are in the *Yab-Yum,* that is, they are in union with their consorts. Vairocana in the centre is white. Akṣobhya as Vajrasattva in the east is blue. Ratnasambhava in the south is yellow. Amitābha in the west is red. Amoghasiddhi in the north is green. Each of them is accompanied by two goddesses and two Bodhisattvas.

The Six Buddhas of the six existences *(ṣaḍ-gati)* in which living beings transmigrate from one to the other, are shown standing with their characteristic colours and attributes. The six worlds are of gods and *asuras*, animals and men, pretas and hell.

The second *maṇḍala* has 58 wrathful deities that dawn from the eighth to the fourteenth day. These flame-haloed, blood-drinking deities are the changed aspect of the former peaceful deities. They issue from the brain centre, the thousand-petalled lotus *(sahasrāra) cakra.* Terror arises in the case of an ordinary deceased who has not had yogic training. One who knows that all appearances are unreal, does not experience the fears of the Bardo. He is reborn among men, or in a paradise, or attains *nirvāṇa* depending on the degree of his Realisation. The blood is a symbol of *samsaric* existence. Seeing the blood-drinking deities, the devotee can realise that they are the personifications of his own propensities of thirsting for life.

The five Herukas embrace their respective consorts or Krodheśvarī and have three faces, six hands and four feet each. Each of the pairs treads Māras under their feet, symbolising the treading on *samsaric* existence, whose renunciation is a prerequisite of reincarnation in a better existence.

The eight Gaurima Goddesses emerge from various quarters of the brain.The twenty-eight animal-headed *yoginīs* are in the outermost rim of the *maṇḍala.* Bearing various weapons, issuing from the east, south, west and north of 'thine own' brain, they come to dazzle. The fearful and terrifying visions are one's own thought forms, that become illusions and one wanders back to *saṁsāra.* If not terrified one does not wander into *saṁsāra,* one's body is of voidness. Voidness cannot injure voidness. Knowing that the emanations of intellectual faculties exist not in reality, all fear and terror is self-dissipated, and the *samādhi* of bliss and luminosity is attained.

Masters, Mystics & Kings

Sixteen Arhats

Śākyamuni Buddha selected sixteen Arhats from his disciples and asked them to stay in the world and protect the teachings till the descent of Maitreya, for the benefit of future beings. Arhats symbolise the spatial diffusion of *Dharma,* as well as its continuity in the period between the two Buddhas, the Buddha of our era and the Future Buddha.

Arhats have travelled the Eightfold Path, succeeded in placing themselves beyond the wheel of transmigration, and are free from all attachment to existence. They have passed through various degrees of saintship and have become 'venerable' in years and in wisdom: visible in their depiction in paintings, according to the *Nandimitra-avadāna* on the Duration of *Dharma.* In the Chinese tradition, the manner of representation is grotesque but expressive in its caricature. The Buddha is surrounded by sixteen Arhats or Apostles of Buddhism. Though they have come to the end of the Path, they do not enter *nirvāṇa* in order to give perfection to others. They symbolise the diffusion of *Dharma* in time and space. This scroll is the first of a set of two depicting eight Arhats and the householder Hva-śaṅ:

Vajrīputra	Bhadra	Vanavāsin
Cūḍapanthaka	Aṅgaja	Kanakavatsa
Hva-śaṅ	Ajita	Kālika

At the bottom is Bhadra, sitting with his right hand in the attitude of explaining the *Dharma,* while the left is in the *mudrā* of meditation. He lives on an island in the Yamuna River. He is responsible for the reincarnation of persons who are born to serve sentient beings. He symbolises preaching Dharma to lead disciples on the correct path.

The second square has Cūḍapanthaka at the top. He is represented seated, with his hands in a meditative posture, which means the elimination of internal and external detrimental elements. He is meditating on Mount Gṛdhrakūṭa, so that living beings can be freed from mental and physical sufferings.

At the bottom is Aṅgaja. He carries a fly-whisk which rests on his right shoulder. A monk approaches him with an incense-burner. This happens on Mount Gandhamādana (*gandha* means fragrance). He lives on Mount Kailash surrounded by a large entourage of Arhats. According to legend, he preached Buddhism to the children of the gods. The children, in place of thanks, offered him lots of incense-burners and fly-whisks. After blessing the children, he took a fly-whisk and an incense-burner in his hands. His blessings protect people from disease and misery.

Another scroll illustrates the remaining eight Arhats and householder Dharmatāla:

FACING PAGE: *8 of the 16* Arhats *or disciples of the Buddha.*

Piṇḍola-bharadvāja	Nāgasena	Gopaka
Panthaka	Bakula	Abheda
Kanaka-bharadvāja	Rāhula	Dharmatāla

Piṇḍola-bharadvāja is derived from the name of a village in the Kosala Kingdom at the Buddha's time. His characteristics are a book in the right hand and a bowl for alms on the left palm in the *samādhi-mudrā.* The bowl represents his miraculous power of granting the wishes of his devotees. He is in charge of the Apara-Godānīya region. His voice is like the roar of a lion. He was prone to exhibit his magical powers, and was rebuked by the Buddha for floating in the air in a sandalwood bowl over the heads of a crowd. Each Arhat has been assigned a quarter of the world, dispersed over the globe. Arhats will watch over and care for the *Dharma* until Maitreya appears as a Buddha.

Arhats do not have definitive attributes which makes their identification a matter of conjecture. Ajita is in the *samādhi-mudrā* of intense meditation, while Kanakavatsa holds a string of precious stones. These specific characteristics are sometimes generalised. Ajita has both his hands folded in the *anjali-mudrā,* while the hands of Kanakavatsa are clearly in the manner of holding a chain of jewels. Both his hands, though covered, are in the gesture of meditation *(samādhi-mudrā).* The name means 'Invincible,' 'Unconquered.' He comes from a wealthy family of Śrāvastī. At first a Brahmin sage, he was ordained by the Buddha himself. He is absorbed in meditation and his eyebrows have grown very long. The Buddha regarded him the most fortunate of all Arhats for he could inspire moral discipline and *samādhi* in whoever saw him.

Two Arhats—Vanavāsin and Vajrīputra—have the right hand in the *tarjanī-mudrā* of threatening, while the left holds a fly-whisk A person is shown offering medicines to Vajrīputra. He dwells in Siṁhala-dvīpa, the Island of Jewels. He preaches to celestial beings who live on sweet fragrance and music. He received a fly-whisk as a token of their devotion. The gesture of his hand assures people protection from evil spirits. He symbolises liberation from negative causes.

Vanavāsin dwells in a cave on the Saptaparṇī Mountain. His right hand is in the *tarjanī mudrā,* while the left holds a fly-whisk. He was a native of Śrāvastī and had heard the *Dharma* from the Buddha himself. The cool hermitage of leaves he has chosen to live in indicates that the world at large is a hot place because of the existence of passion. Everlasting peace is attainable by dispassionate meditation in passive solitude in the forest. He represents victory over delusion and prevention of man-made or natural harms. A disciple stands with folded hands, and peacocks recall the woods near Mount Saptaparṇī.

Tibetan texts specify three styles of representing the Arhats: the Indian manner, as monks, introduced by one of the three pandits who accompanied Atīśa, the Chinese and the Tibetan.

Six Jewels of Buddhism

The role of disciples, apostles, transcreators of Sanskrit *sūtra*s into Tibetan, and the *Dharma* Kings in the spread of Buddhism has been recorded in scrolls and sculptures. Arhats were worshipped because they had postponed their *nirvāṇa,* and stayed in the world for the happiness of gods and men. The record of the teacher, Nandimitra gives the lives of the sixteen Arhats. The Arhats came into full glory as protective saints. Tibetan art celebrates the Six Jewels (gyendruk) of Buddhism who initiated different systems of thought. They are:

(i) Nāgārjuna and Āryadeva who received the *Prajñā-pāramitā* or Transcendental Philosophy from a Nāga princess.
(ii) Asaṅga and Vasubandhu who received *Yogācāra* or *Vijñānavāda* philosophy from Maitreya
(iii) Diṅnāga and Dharmakīrti who are great masters of logic. Kṣitigarbha is their presiding deity.

Representation of historical personages provides a rich source for *thaṅka* scrolls. Beginning with the depiction of the disciples of the Buddha, Maitreya with Asaṅga and Vasubandhu in the 5th century, we come to the sixteen Arhats and the 84 Siddhas. As *Guru Yoga* gained in importance, their paintings or images came into greater vogue. The lineages of transmission of various *tantra*s were handed down with meticulous care to retain the authenticity of tradition. Hagiographic scrolls as those of Padmasambhava, Milarepa and Tsoṅ-kha-pa are masterpieces of narrative art. The incarnational series of the Dalai and Panchen Lamas and other great masters are the flow of *Dharma.*

Nāgārjuna (Tibetan: Klu-sgrub) has an aureole which has five snakes. He has the *uṣṇī sa* or protuberance over the head like Buddha Śākyamuni and is of white complexion (*arjuna* 'white'). His hands are in the *Dharmacakra-mudrā* of promulgating the *Dharma,* as his revelation of the *Prajñā-pāramitā* from the *nāga*s is known as the 'Second Turning of the Wheel of *Dharma*', as a corollary to the First Turning by Buddha Śākyamuni. He was born in a wealthy Brahmin family of Vidarbha. To avoid the prediction of a short life, his father made him take to the robes. He studied all the disciplines at Nalanda University under the great sage Rāhulabhadra. Later he was appointed the chief abbot of Nalanda that outshone others institutions as a seat of knowledge and monastic discipline. A great part of his life was spent at Śrīparvata in South

Śūnyatā

Svātantrika and Prāsaṅgika are two systems of the interpretation of the philosophy of non-substantiality or void—*śūnyatā* in Sanskrit. This concept developed in the *Wisdom Sutras* and Nāgārjuna (*c.* 150-250) systematised it in his *Madhyamaka-kārikā*. It originated from dependent origination and the non-existence of self-nature. Dependent origination means that phenomena arise by virtue of their relationship with other phenomena, and have no existence of their own. The message is that the true nature of all phenomena is non-substantiality. Nāgārjuna regards existence and non-existence as extremes and tries to transcend them as the Middle Way. The *Madhyamaka* philosophy bifurcated into two schools: Svātantrika and Prāsaṅgika. The Svātantrika School was founded by Bhāvaviveka (*c.* 490-570) and the Prāsaṅgika by Buddhapālita (*c.* 470-540). Bhāvaviveka wrote *The Lamp of Wisdom*, a commentary on Nāgārjuna. He based his system on Buddhist logic developed by Diṅnāga. His method was syllogism-based *(svatantra)* to establish valid propositions, in contradiction to the reduction *ad absurdum* of the Prāsaṅgikas who sought only the contradictions in the postulates of the opponents.

Bhāvaviveka was born in a royal family of South India, and excelled in debate. He headed some fifty monasteries in the Dhānyakaṭaka region. He formulated a synthesis of *Mādhyamika* dialectics and logical conventions. His works are preserved only in Tibetan translations. He is the forerunner of the literary style of *Siddhānta* (Tibetan: grub-mthah), which became popular in Tibetan academics. His work on the early schisms within Buddhist ranks as one of the most reliable sources for the early history of Buddhism. He admits degrees of reality and levels of insight dependent on spiritual maturity.

India where archaeological discoveries revealed his dynamic abilities. Nāgārjuna's formulation of *śūnyatā* had far-reaching effects on the thought of Asia.

Bhavya (Tibetan: Legs-ldan; right) is the founder of the Svātantrika system. On the top left is Nāgārjuna and opposite him is Sahaja Saṁvara, who appeared to Bhavya in a vision. At the bottom is Four-armed Mahākāla, dark blue (whence the epithet bya-rog-can—raven-coloured), and dancing on a white corpse.

Diṅnāga (Tibetan: Phyogs-glaṅ; p. 157) is one of the Six Jewels of Mahāyāna Buddhism (Tibetan: Rgyan drug). A celebrated master of Buddhist logic, he flourished in the 5th century. Born of a Brahmin family of Siṁhavaktra near Kanchi, he became a pupil of Vasubandhu and completed his studies at Nalanda University. His most renowned work is the *Pramāṇa-samuccaya,* one of the keenest and subtlest works of Buddhist speculation. He holds that 'intuition trained through intellect leads to the realisation of Absolute Reality.'

Dharmakīrti (p. 156) is one of the Six Jewels of Mahāyāna and is termed 'the sun among dialecticians.' He lived in the 7th century AD, a contemporary of Sroṅ-btsan-sgam-po, and the Chinese monk, I-tsing, who speaks highly of him. He was born in a Brahmin family of Cola (northern Tamil Nadu) and became versed in Buddhist *sūtras*

ABOVE: *Bhavya or Bhāvaviveka was an exponent of* Mādhyamika *philosophy. He founded a new school of the interpretation of* Mādhyamika—*the Svātantrika School. He lived around* AD *490-570. The* Mādhyamika*s avoided the two extremes of Absolute Reality and the total unreality of phenomena. Nāgārjuna is in the top left-hand corner.*

and *dhāraṇīs* at Nalanda, under Dharmapāla. Under Īśvarasena, a disciple of Diṅnāga, he studied logic. He not only became the continuator of Diṅnāga's system, but far surpassed his teacher with his monumental works.

The eighty-four *siddhas* of the Indian esoteric tradition are those who have attained supreme realisation *(siddhi)* through *sādhanā*. They have become transcendental *(lokottara)* in being one with cosmic consciousness. On the earthly *(laukika)* level they have acquired miraculous powers. Among them is Naropa, the great *siddha*, a pupil of Tilopa, and an ancestor of the Kargyupa order. Naropa dominates with his powerful presence. Both his hands hold a

ABOVE: *Diṅnāga, who lived around* AD *480-540 developed the epistemological approach in* yogācāra. *He worked at Nalanda for a long time. He admits two touchstones of knowledge—direct perception and logical conclusion.*

FACING PAGE: *Dharmakīrti was an outstanding logician who studied at Nalanda. His works treat the nature of knowledge, and its relation to the external world. His* Nyāya-bindu *is a concise guide to logic.*

cranium or *kapāla;* he wears ornaments of bone, and is tied with a *yoga-paṭṭa* to sustain the yogic posture. Paintings represent him in various stages of his spiritual life: first he is seated on a deer-skin, with a *tridaṇḍī* and vase *kamaṇḍalu* tucked into the earth nearby. Thereafter, he sits on the deer-skin with a cranium, after the Vajravārāhī initiation. In both stages, he has no bone-ornaments.

Naropa came from a family of wine-sellers, but gave up his family profession. He earned his living by gathering wood. Once he heard of a very wise man Tilopa. He exchanged his load of wood for a black antelope's pelt and wore it as the dress of a *yogin.* He went in search of Tilopa and finally met him on the road. He circumambulated Tilopa and said: 'O Guru, are you in good health?' Tilopa began to thrash him. For twelve years he served him as a guru, who spoke to him only in anger and struck him, but Naropa's faith was unshaken. One day, Naropa was begging alms near a wedding place. He got a green sweet *patasha* with eighty-four ingredients. The guru was delighted to eat it. He initiated Naropa into the visualisation of Vajravārāhī. He meditated for six months, obtained *siddhi,* and became famous everywhere. Finally he rose bodily into the paradise of *ḍākinīs.*

The asceticism of the *siddha*s spread to Tibet with Marpa, who was initiated by Naropa. The Six Laws of Naropa (chos-drug) became the fundamental text of the Kargyupa order and a vast literature crytallised about them. The Six Laws are a summary of *Haṭha Yoga* principles in six steps.

The corpulent, dark and sky-clad great *siddha* Virūpa (p. 160) was born in Tripura during the reign of King Devapāla. He was ordained in the monastic university of Somapuri. While young, he was granted the empowerment of Vajravārāhī. He recited twenty million times her *mantra* for twelve years. When he did not receive even a dream omen to signify progress, he threw away his rosary into a toilet. At the time of the evening worship when he had no rosary, a *ḍākinī* appeared and put his rosary into his hand, and advised him to abandon all wandering and critical thought. He practised the spiritual discipline of Vajravārāhī for another twelve years and attained the Supreme Realisation of *Mahāmudrā.* But he became accustomed to eating meat and drinking alcohol. So he was expelled from the monastery. He approached the large lake near the monastery and set off across the lake, flitting from one lotus leaf to the other, and reached the other shore. When the inmates of Somapuri saw this they were filled with remorse and touched his feet with the deepest devotion. He abandoned the life of a monk and became a *yogin.*

Virūpa who meditated in a tavern over a dozen glasses of wine, turned back the Ganga River, and stopped the sun, is the forefather of the

FACING PAGE: *Naropa (*AD *1016-1100) is the best-known Indian* siddha *who trasmitted the* Mahāmudrā *teachings through Marpa. He was in Nalanda and a contemporary of Atiśa. His 'Six* Dharmas*'* (chos-drug) *constitute the central doctrines of the Kagyupa denomination.*

Sakyapa denomination. His religious path began with Mahāyāna and culminated in Vajrayāna of the *Hevajra Tantra*. He says:

> Mine is the spontaneous reality disposed by
> the Magnificent Symbol.
> Just abiding in things as they are, not thinking,
> not achieving, no self,
> Saved from the pit of nihilism of self-aware
> existential experience,
> Saved from the heavens of eternalism by
> absolute detachment,
> This reality is consummation of perfect awareness
> and pure delight.

Padmasambhava

Like a Second Buddha, Padmasambhava (p. 163) came into the world, west of Bodhgaya, in Oḍḍiyāna by apparitional birth. As the HRĪḤ went out from the heart of Amitābha and settled on a lotus flower, an eight-year-old boy, endowed with all knowledge, was born. King Indrabhūti dispatched his minister to find out the miraculous emanation. The minister found a child of eight, seated on the lotus, encircled by rainbow auras and *ḍākinī*s. When the child was brought to the court and the King asked him, he replied: 'My father is Wisdom. My mother is Voidness. Mine is the country of *Dharma*. I am sustained by clarity and perplexity.' He was Padmasambhava. After that he was seen by King Indrabhūti, who invited him to his palace and adopted him as his son. Subsequently he crowned him as king. The people thereupon called him Padmavajra and Rājaśekhara. When he grew up, he realised that the world was devoid of reality, and renounced his kingship. He then went to the cremation ground near Bodhgaya, which was a famous resort of *yogin*s, and gained emancipation of the mind through the higher practices.

King Khri-sroṅ-lde-btsan, who reigned from AD 756–797, invited Padmasambhava to help in the re-establishment of Buddhism. Padmasambhava set out for Tibet. First, he went to Nepal, and remained there for three months as a guest of the king. At the time of his departure from Nepal, *ḍākinī*s and other spiritual beings begged him not to go to Tibet, but the guru said that he must go as the time had come to subdue the evil spirits.

He arrived in Tibet about three-and-a-half-months later, in AD 747, at the beginning of spring. He went to Tibet twice and stayed there for some years. His principal task was to demonstrate the superiority of the miracle-working power of Buddhism to that of Bon. He adapted the new faith to the psychology of the Tibetans and paved the way for its rapid spread throughout the land.

FACING PAGE: *Virūpa is recognised as the founder of the Sakyapa order. He was a master of the Cakrasaṁvara and Hevajra lineages. Initiated into the* maṇḍala *of Hevajra by Nairātmā, he transmitted the doctrine of 'Path and Fruit' (lam-ḥbras) based on the* Hevajra-Tantra, *to the Sakyapas.*

Padmasambhava sits with his legs crossed in the *vajrāsana.* He holds a *vajra* in the right hand and a skull-cup in the left. The magic staff or *khaṭvāṅga* rests in the crook of his left arm. The three are characteristics of a great exorcist, of an eminent tantric master who vanquishes demons. By his magical power, which none could withstand, he subdued the demons or enemies of Buddhism in Tibet, converted them and transformed them into protectors of the *Dharma.* The new world order was symbolised by the construction of the Samye Monastery in 749, consecrated in the presence of Padmasambhava. Samye was to be the continuing symbol of Tibet as the Buddha-kṣetra. He directed the translation of *sūtras* and *mantras* brought from India. While Śāntarakṣita represented argument and logic, Padmasambhava was the trans-logical thaumaturge. It put the final seal on the submission of the gods and demons he had vanquished, and Buddhism was established irrevocably in Tibet.

King Ral-pa-can

The most outstanding among human *Dharma* Kings are the three great kings of the early Yarlung period, who ruled from the 7th to the 9th centuries AD. They were Sroṅtbtsan-sgam-po, an incarnation of Avalokiteśvara who ruled from AD 618 to 649, Khri Sroṅ-lde-brtsan, an incarnation of Mañjuśrī who reigned from AD 755 to 797, and Khri Ral-pa-can (p. 164) an incarnation of Vajrapāṇi whose rule extended from AD 815 to 838. Their reigns mark the rise, zenith and persecution of Buddhism. As incarnations of the three Buddhist deities, Avalokiteśvara, Mañjuśrī and Vajrapāṇi, they became paradigms for the Buddhist rule of the Sakyapas and others, culminating in the Dalai Lamas.

In Ral-pa-can's reign temples were embellished with statues and paintings. The Buddhist monk Bande Yon-tan served as Ral-pa-can's prime minister. He invited three Indian pandits, Śīlendrabodhi, Dānaśīla, and Jinamitra, to Central Tibet and provided them with two prominent translators, Ka-ba Dpal-brstegs and Chogro Lui Gyaltsen. They standardised the terms used for translating Buddhist concepts from Sanskrit. The first dictionary, called the *Mahāvyutpatti,* was compiled at that time.

After ascending the throne, Ral-pa-can sent troops under the command of Hrangje Tsen towards the Chinese border. Buddhists in China and Tibet sought mediation, and finally both countries sent representatives to the border. A meeting was held in 821 and a peace treaty was concluded. This devout king was assassinated by his elder brother Glaṅ-dar-ma in 838 and Tibet saw a period of repression of Buddhism.

FACING PAGE: *Padmasambhava was invited by King Khri Sroṅ-lde-brtsan to subdue the demons so that the construction of the first monastery of Samye in Tibet could be completed. He is revered as the Guru Rinpoche 'Precious Guru', who converted Tibet into a realm of* Dharma.

Milarepa, the Great Yogin

Milarepa (AD 1040–1123; p. 167) is a poet who wrote according to his own inspiration. When he breaks from esoteric abstruseness or technicalities of *yoga,* he soars on the wings of fancy in perfect purity, in the fire of an unquenched mystical ardour. He instills new life in the style, structure and form of the Dohā songs of the *siddhas*, who are his inspiration. With personal touches, rare in Tibetan hieratic poetry, his genius gave to Tibet its first poesy—sensitive, warm, lyrical, not choked by dogmatic reminiscences. All sects of Tibetan Buddhism hold him in the highest reverence, as one who soars into spiritual space wherein all doctrines merge. Milarepa dwelt in caves.

He had a single possession: a pitcher for water. One day it fell and broke into a hundred fragments. Instead of despairing, he sang to the pitcher: 'You were the only thing I had. Now that you are broken, you have become a Lama, and preached an admirable sermon on the impermanence of things.' The ascetic Milarepa had incandescent inner experiences in the white snows of the Himalayas. He grew to manhood surrounded by implacable hate and excessive love. He knew poverty and riches, black magic and revenge. His life story, written by his pupil Ras-chuṅ, is full of fisticuffs and crime reporting, visions and metaphysics, vivid with human warmth, which is compelling even to a modern reader. He founds a master in Marpa, the translator of Sanskrit texts, temperamental, with the spirit of lightning and the violence of a storm.

At initiation, Marpa gave his pupil the maxim: 'Be ardent, fly the banner of perfection.' Milarepa, the naked hermit, owned no books and ever singing he moved from cave to cave. Once hunters arrived at his cave to whom he sang: 'The horse that is my spirit flies like the wind...' Milarepa is seated among blue-green cliffs, tumbling waterfalls, colourful red lotuses, in an intriguing but colourful landscape of the holy Himalayas, himself ringed with a diaphanous rainbow-like halo.

Pha-dam-pa-saṅs-rgyas, the Great Siddha

Pha-dam-pa-saṅs-rgyas (p. 168) is represented as a teacher of the Gcod tradition dealing with the process of thought. He holds the drum in his right and bell in his left hand. His other representation is as the originator of the zhi-byed wherein he is in a squatting position indicative of his practice of *caṇḍī* or 'inner heat' *yoga.*

Gcod is one of the two branches of the school founded by the Indian ascetic Pha-dam-pa who died in AD 1117. Gcod means to cut away the false attachments to an ego *(ātman)* by offering one's body

FACING PAGE: *King Ral-pa-can invited the Indian teachers Śīlendrabodhi, Dānaśīla and Jinamitra to Tibet. They standardised the terminology for the translation of Buddhist texts with the help of Tibetan masters. King Ral-pa-can was killed in* AD *836 in a court intrigue aimed at establishing the Bon religion.*

to demons. It implies cutting through the thinking process by the use of meditation techniques.

Zhi-byed is the second branch of the school of Pha-dam-pa. It means 'to pacify suffering'. The objective of this school is the liberation of living beings from suffering in all its forms.

Pha-dam-pa was the son of the jewel-merchant Vīryavarman and his mother Barasaha came from a family of incense-makers. He hailed from South India. He mastered grammar and other lesser sciences in his childhood. He was ordained by Kṣemadeva and became learned in texts on monastic discipline or Vinaya. The creative effort towards Enlightenment became in him surging waves by the inspiration of Dharmakīrti.

He obtained the profound precepts from fifty-four male and female *siddhas*. He practised meditation at Seṅ-ge-rdzoṅ, Vajrāsana, Svayambhū-caitya, cemeteries of South India, and several other places. He obtained worldly *siddhis*—he found an eye ointment applying which one can see treasures underground, the power to fly through space, and so on. In respect of the sublime *siddhis* he attained the Path of Illumination (mthoṅ-lam), as well as deep knowledge and realisation of *Mahāmudrā*.

He visited Tibet five times. His second visit was via Kashmir, and the third through Nepal. During the fifth visit to Tibet, he proceeded from there to China where he spent twelve years. He returned to Dingri. A Tibetan Kun-dgaḥ asked about the number of disciples invited by him. He replied: 'Can you count the stars in heaven above the plain Dingri?' He settled there with his disciples, and died twenty-one years later in 1117. The Dingri Monastery founded by him exists even now.

Pha-dam-pa was a Buddhist *siddha* who laid the foundations of the Zhi-byed School to liberate living beings from suffering in all forms. When he arrived in Tibet he was taken to be a Śaiva *yogin*. His first teachings were: 'The mind must not grow fond of the body. The body must not grow fond of the mind. Guard the liberty of body and mind, so that each can rest in itself.'

Ma-gcig Lab-sgron-ma

Cutting through the process of thought (gcod), which causes duality of the apparent world, is Ma-gcig Lab-sgron-ma (AD 1055–1149; p. 169). She founded the Gcod tradition, which brings about the pure state of Being by cutting off the discursive process at the root. It brings about the direct insight that nothing exists.

Ma-gcig is Mother (ma) Unique (gcig) invoked by the meditator in his attempt to go beyond human finiteness, to represent the inconceivable and inexpressible. She was born in ad 1055 in Lab in E-yul. Hence her name is Light (sgron-ma) of

FACING PAGE: *Milarepa (AD 1025-1135) is the most famous poet-saint of Tibet, who wore cotton robes of an ascetic. His guru Marpa imposed cruel difficulties on him, before giving him the teachings. His spiritual songs are a source of inspiration. Clad only in a thin cotton cloth in icy mountain caves, he practised gtum.mo or inner heat.*

ABOVE: *Ma-gcig Lab-sgron-ma as a white dancing* ḍākinī. *She is known for the* Gcod *tradition of meditative and ritual practices based on the* Prajñā-pāramitā. *Through the introduction of* Gcod *she gave a magnificent scale to the goal of Enlightenment.* Gcod *brings about the pure state of Being by cutting off the discursive process.*

FACING PAGE: *Pha-dam-pa and his disciple Ma-gcig Lab-sgron-ma initiated a system of transformative visualisations termed 'cutting off'* (Gcod).

Lab. One of the most outstanding woman saints of Tibet, she is a disciple of Pha-dam-pa Saṅs-rgyas, the Indian mystic who went to Tibet five times. He met her on his third journey to Tibet. He introduced the doctrine of Zhi-byed and the practice of Gcod techniques. Zhi-byed emphasizes the calming of the mind as the essence of the path of *Prajñā-pāramitā,* while Gcod is the meditative path that leads to spontaneous detachment from the ego. Ma-gcig Lab-sgron-ma is an incarnation of the three goddesses, Prajñāpāramitā, Vajravārāhī and Khro-ma Nag-mo, or Blue-Black Fierce Kālī, all of them important in the Gcod tradition.

Pāramitā is the system of teaching that forms its basis, and hence the body of Ma-gcig has the white colour of Prajñā-pāramitā. She is in the dancing posture of Vajravārāhī. In the right hand she holds a *ḍamaru* or drum to bring to submission macabre and gruesome beings like the *ḥdre,* while the bell in the left hand symbolises oneness with wisdom.

Tsoṅ-kha-pa

Tsoṅ-kha-pa Blo-bzaṅ-grags-pa (AD 1357–1419; p. 172) was born in the Tibetan valley of Tsoṅ-kha, hence his epithet which has assumed the proportions of a proper name. He was born in AD 1357 in a house overshadowed by a tree each of whose leaves is assumed to have had an image or the *arapacana* *mantra* inscribed. Around it came up the Kumbum Jambaling monastery. Tsoṅ-kha-pa founded the order (lugs) of 'The Virtuous' (dge), the Gelukpa (written Dge-lugs-pa) School, which imposed strict monastic discipline of celibacy, abstention from alcohol and advocated vegetarianism. The school spread fast throughout Tibet by the prodigious capacities and tireless labours of the founder who impressed the life and thought of the land by his singular philological and exegetical acumen and immense learning in dogmatics, ritual as well as theological subtleties. As monks of his school wore pointed yellow caps, the denomination came to be known as the Yellow School or Yellow Hats.

With the ascendancy of the Gelukpas, Tsoṅ-kha-pa was considered to be a Mañjuśrī who had taken the vow of a being embodied for the well-being of suffering creatures. He is actually represented with the attributes of Mañjuśrī: the flaming sword of wisdom *(prajñā-khaḍga)* to dispel ignorance placed on a lotus whose stem is held in the right hand and the book of Transcendental Wisdom, the *Prajñā-pāramitā,* on the left-hand lotus. He is further represented as a sleek-faced young man like his spiritual sire Mañjuśrī Kumāra-bhūta, the Perennial Youth. He wears the characteristic yellow cap with long lappets over the ears falling over the shoulders. His robes are of saffron red colour. His hands are in the *Dharmacakra-mudrā* of

Gelukpa

Gelukpa is the main and the last denomination of Tibetan Buddhism. It means 'School of the Virtuous'. It was enunciated by Tsoṅ-kha-pa (AD 1357-1419), whose charisma made an impression on his contemporaries. He had a following of high families and gifted disciples. His two main disciples were Rgyal-tshab (AD 1364-1432) and Mkhas.grub (AD 1385-1438). The Gelukpa tradition emphasizes the systematic study and practice of *sutra*s and *tantra*s as systematised by Tsoṅ-kha-pa on the basis of earlier Kadampa teachings. Secondly, it stresses compliance with the monastic discipline of Vinaya. Gelukpas created large monasteries, like the Tashilhumpo founded in 1445 by Dge-ḥdun-grub (AD 1391-1474), the Drepung constructed by Dge.ḥdun. rgya.mtsho (AD 1475-1542) who was recognised as the second Dalai Lama posthumously. The installation of the Fifth Dalai Lama (AD 1617-1682) as the ruler of the whole of Tibet by the Mongolian Gushri Khan made Gelukpa the dominant tradition. The rule of the Dalai Lamas brought the resources of the state at their disposal. The three monasteries around Lhasa became international seats of learning as well as wielded immense political power. The doctrinal system of the Gelukpas is based on the works of Tsoṅ-kha-pa and his two disciples Rgyal-tshab and Mkhas.grub. Having had a vision of Mañjūśrī, Tsoṅ-kha-pa wrote his luminous commentary on *Mādhyamika* philosophy and detailed meditation manuals. Tsoṅ-kha-pa shows that *samādhi* can be achieved by dwelling in tranquility *(śamatha)* and through special insight *(vipaśyanā). Tantra*s show techniques for realising this state of equilibrium. Attaining the state of Enlightenment *(bodhicitta)* leads to insight into true reality.

ABOVE: *Tsoṅ-kha-pa studied all branches of knowledge under several teachers of the Karmapa, Sakyapa and Kadampa orders. His four great actions were: restoration of the image of Maitreya; proper observance of the Vinaya; establishment of the new year's festival Monlam, and construction of monasteries.*

preaching, of which the left hand lies in the lap with an alms-bowl to signify that he is the second Buddha Śākyamuni. This is the epithet which grew along with his legend for which prophecies were traced back to ancient texts assumed to have foreseen the advent of the Master.

Several series of illustrations on the life of Tsoṅ-kha-pa are known. The most renowned of them are the 15 Tashilhunpo woodcuts, containing 203 episodes. They were drawn by Ḥjamd-byaṅs-bzhad-pa in the 18th century. The episodes depicted in one of the scrolls are as follows (The numbers indicate the depiction of the following episodes in the life of Tsoṅ-kha-pa):

68, 69	70	71	72	
67	65	66	75	76a
64				76
63	Tsoṅ-kha-pa			
61				62
				58
57	55, 56		54	51, 52

51. Pondering over the Pramāṇa-vārttika an extraordinary knowledge of its intuitive sense arose in him.

52. In Mal-gro Lha-luṅ, Tsoṅ-kha-pa applied himself to intensive study at the school of the master Bsod-nams-grags-pa.

54. At Snar-thaṅ he studied with the Lotsava Don-bzaṅ his commentary on the *Pramāṇa-vārttika.*

55. In Bo-don, at E monastery he listened to *Mādhyamika,* logic and other disciplines (at Chos-dbaṅs school).

56. At the school of the lotsava Nam-mkhaḥ-bzaṅ-po, he learnt Kāvyādarśa on rhetoric.

57. He and his teacher went to Sa-skya where he studied the *Pramāṇa-vārttika, Abhidharma* and *Vinaya.*

58. He went to Gun-thaṅ and studied subjects other than the *Prajñā-pāramitā* at the monasteries of Gsaṅ-phu, Rtse-thaṅ, among others.

61. In Yar-kluṅs he obtained final vows from Tshul-khrims-rin-chen who presided over the ceremony. Śes-rab-mgon-po took part in it as preceptor (las-dpon) and Bsod-nams-rdo-rje as esoteric teacher (gsaṅ ston).

62. In Gadan-sa-thel he met the Spyan-sṅa Grags-

ABOVE: *Life of Tsoṅ-kha-pa or 'Man from the Onion Valley'. He created the most important doctrinal tradition of Buddhism by founding the Gelukpa order.*

pa-byaṅ-chub, gave him the book *Legs-bśad-gser-ḥphreṅ,* a commentary on the *Abhisamayālaṅkāra.*

65. Led by Tsha-go-dpon-po, he went to Lhasa where he paid homage to Avalokiteśvara.

66. From Tshal he came to Bde-ba-can and expounded sacred books.

67. In Bya-yul, in Upper Dbus, he taught the *Prajñā-pāramitā* to seventy doctors of divinity.

68. Once more he returned to Tshal to continue the Legs-bśad-gser-ḥphreṅ (the inscription is illegible).

70. In Skyor-mo-luṅ, he lectured to several *piṭakadhara*s on a number of minor and major *śāstra*s.

71. During the summer retreat at Bde-ba-can, he gave discourses on sacred treatises to the gathering of monks convoked by Blo-gsal-rgya-mtsho.

72. In Mtsho-smad of Stod-luṅ, he applied himself to the study of the *Kālacakra.*

74. Grags-pa-rin-chen, the chief of Rdziṅ-ji took him to Yar-luṅ Smon-mkhar where he delivered many discourses.

75. In the Rigs-lṅa-lha-khaṅ (a temple dedicated to the five mystical families) he explained several *śāstra*s to proficient monks.

76a. Sarasvatī favoured him with her patronage and became his guiding goddess.

These events cover the life of Tsoṅ-kha-pa since he was twenty-two years upto his thirty-second year.

FACING PAGE: *Tsoṅ-kha-pa presented his teachings in two major treatises: the* Lam-rim-chen-mo *or 'Great Discourse on the Stages of Enlightenment', and the* Sṅags-rim-chen-mo *or the 'Great Discourse on the Esoteric* Mantra*s.'*

Medical Thaṅkas

Maṇḍala of Gyuzhi

Naimittika deities are those invoked for specific purposes *(nimitta):* like health and wealth. The Rin-lhan of the Panchen Lama is divided into 23 sections. Section 10 details deities of long life, section 11 comprises deities that bestow wisdom, and section 17 contains wealth-giving deities. For example, deities to prolong life are Amitāyus, along with Uṣṇīṣavijayā and Amaravajradevī.

The basic text of Tibetan medicine is the *Gyuzhi* or *Four Tantras* by Candranandana, translated into Tibetan by Jinamitra and Dānaśīla with Yeshede and others in the 9th century. It is still the fundamental classic of Tibetan medicine. The Buddha appeared as the Medicine Buddha or Bhaiṣajyaguru for the sake of the sick, and future disciples. He taught the *Gyuzhi* at the Sudarśana (Tibetan: Tanaduk) palace of Indra on Mount Sumeru. The Buddha spent four years in the medicine jungle in the Sudarśana palace. The Medicine Buddha fell into the *samādhi* called 'expelling 404 diseases'. He taught the *Gyuzhi* with its 156 chapters.

It was written down in 5900 stanzas with beryl ink on sheets of pure gold. The original is believed to be kept in the place of *ḍākinīs*. The Regent of the Fifth Dalai Lama wrote a comprehensive commentary on the *Gyuzhi* of Candranandana. This is called the *Lapis Lazuli Commentary* (Tibetan: Vaiḍūryā-sṅon-po). Traditional colleges of medicine in Tibet, Mongolia and as far as Siberia had illustrated scrolls of the complete text. This 'diamond healing' of Tibet is a holistic approach to man as a healthy being in body and mind, and disease as a disturbance of this homostasis.

There are three types of medicine *maṇḍalas*: (i) the *Gyuzhi* with Bhaiṣajyaguru as the central deity in the garden of herbs, minerals and animals; (ii) Amitāyus as the central deity and (iii) Bhaiṣayaguru represented by his *sūtra* or scripture.

An entire series of paintings is devoted to the fundamental treatise on medicine, the *Gyuzhi* read with its commentary *Vaiḍūryā-sṅon-po* (Blue Lapis Lazuli). It comprises four parts: root or fundamental, explanatory, instruction and concluding treatises. It was adapted from a Sanskrit original by the Kashmiri physician Candranandana in the 8th century AD. He assisted Vairocanarakṣita in the translation. Vairocanarakṣita is a famous translator who lived during the reign of King Khri Sroṅ-lde-btsan.

It was commented upon at length by the Regent Saṅs-rgyas-rgya-mtsho (AD 1653–1705), who founded the Chakpori Medical College at Lhasa. His major contribution lies in that he decreed that each district and each big monastery should train a doctor of its own. These were the beginning of public health in Tibet.

FACING PAGE: *The* maṇḍala *of Gyuzhi with Bhaiṣajyaguru in the centre, surrounded by plants, animals and stones used in pharmacopeia.*

The central deity in the *maṇḍala*-palace is Amitāyus, with the vase of ambrosia, topped by leaves of the tree aśoka, which means 'without suffering' and symbolises a long span of healthy life without diseases. Rays of light emanate from the heart of the deity, as the *sādhaka* physician invokes him to adjust the vibrational harmony of the subtle and gross body. Medicines are placed in a cranium *(kapāla)* over which sits White Amitāyus.

The light from the heart of the Divine goes to the realms of all the Buddhas, Bodhisattvas, goddesses, and to the six existences. The essence of all is drawn into the heart of the deity. The medicines are duly sanctified and endowed with full divine potency. It becomes the medicine of *Dharma*.

In the right hand corner is the Vaiḍūrya Buddha, the mystical transformation of the Buddha who gave the teachings that have come down to us as the *Gyuzhi*. He resides in the middle of heaven, in a transparent crystal palace where he is enthroned on a seat of lapis lazuli *(vaiḍūrya)*. Lapis lazuli symbolises medicine in Buddhism. The Medicine Buddha is translucent, blue in colour, holds the myrobalan *(arura)* plant in his right hand which rests on his knee in the gesture of giving. His left hand rests in the lap and holds an alms bowl filled with healing nectar. He expounded these teachings in the Sudarśana Paradise, where he projected two emanations: the first, the sage Rig-paḥi-ye-śes: an emanation of the mind of the Medicine Buddha, and the second, the sage Yid-las-skyes: an emanation of the speech of the Medicine Buddha. The *Gyuzhi* is recorded in the form of a dialogue between these two sages.

Bhaiṣajyaguru

Bhaiṣajyaguru (Tibetan: Sman-bla) is the god of medicine, the physican of human passions, the unfailing healer of the ills of *saṁsāra*. He is of dark blue colour like lapis lazuli, hence called Vaiḍūryaprabharāja. Blue is well known as Akṣobhya's colour; hence he receives some of the attributes of Akṣobhya who presides over the east. Bhaiṣajyaguru holds the myrobalan in the right hand and the left hand has a pot of medicines. The pot is of lapis lazuli and twelve-sided in form that symbolises his twelve resolutions for helping human beings. His expression is calm and serene, and he does not wear a crown on the head. He is flanked by two Bodhisattvas: Sūryaprabha—Solar Radiance— to the right, and Candraprabha— Lunar Radiance—to the left.

Sixteen Bodhisattvas are shown in vertical panels on his sides. His Twelve Yakṣa Generals are charged to project adepts by his grace. Each of them reigns over one of the twelve parts of the day, and twelve months, while Sūryaprabha and

FACING PAGE: *Bhaiṣajyaguru with his seven emanations. He symbolises the healing quality of Buddhahood. His Eastern Pure Land radiates light to all beings, fulfils their wishes, enables them to maintain the rules of discipline, and so on.*

Candraprabha rule over day and night. The *yakṣa* generals can be seen holding a mongoose. It is the first *thaṅka* of the series illustrating the *Vaiḍūryā-sṅon-po* commentary by Saṅs-rgyas-rgya-mtsho (ad 1620–1705), the regent of the Fifth Dalai Lama. He commented on the fundamental medical text of the *Gyuzhi*.

Bhaiṣajyaguru begins the classical treatise. It depicts the transmission of medicine from Brahmā to the divine physicians, the twin Aśvins. They handed it down to Indra. Indra passed it on to divine sages who brought the science of medicine from the world of gods to that of humans. This was the divine Brahmā system of medicine.

Bhaiṣajyaguru is at the centre of the scroll (p. 179) imparting the *Gyuzhi* to Devas, sages, Arhats and Jīvakas. He sits in the celestial palace in the centre of the city on a mountain. The four gates of the palace are guarded by the four *lokapāla*s: Vaiśravaṇa, Virūpākṣa, Dhṛtarāṣṭra and Virūḍhaka.

All around the celestial palace are the many houses of the city in concentric layout. They are surrounded by gardens of medicinal herbs, pharmaceutical minerals and hot springs. In the outer concentric enclosure are trees as well as animals of medical importance. The animals have Tibetan names.

On the topmost panel are the Buddhas of Medicine. At the bottom is the spiritually created complex: the forest of medicinal trees and animals, with herbs in the next concentric enclosure, a city with villas enclosed by them, and in the very centre Bhaiṣajyaguru proclaiming the science of medicine. The city of medical science is surrounded on four sides by mountains with specially effective medical herbs that heal the 404 disorders of the body. Tibetan medicine, as a transcendental system or 'diamond healing', explores further shores of a holistic approach to man as a healthy being in body and mind, and disease as a disturbance of this homeostasis.

FACING PAGE: *The* maṇḍala *of Bhaiṣajyaguru, in which he is represented by his scripture.*

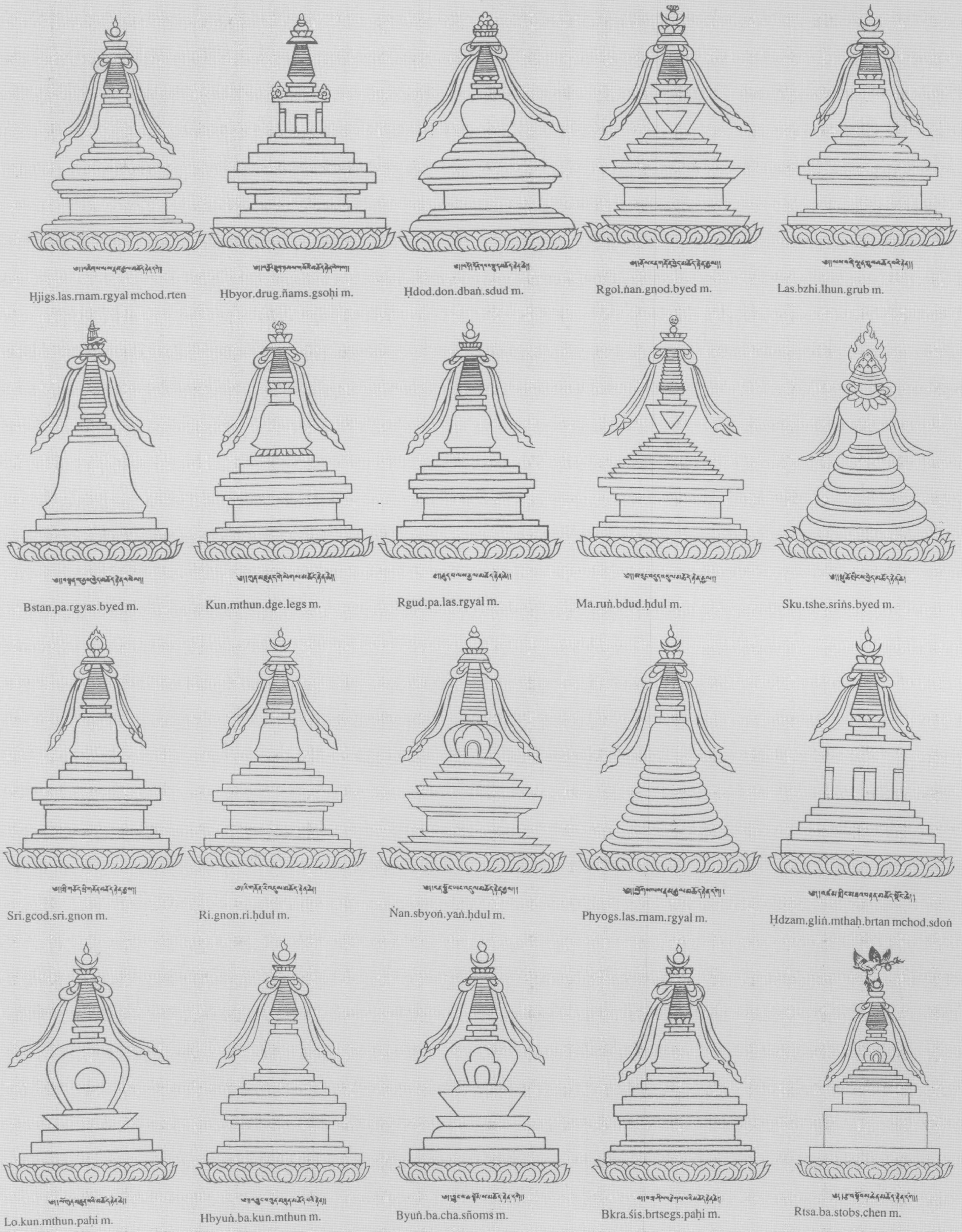
Ḥjigs.las.rnam.rgyal mchod.rten
Ḥbyor.drug.ñams.gsoḥi m.
Ḥdod.don.dbaṅ.sdud m.
Rgol.ṅan.gnod.byed m.
Las.bzhi.lhun.grub m.
Bstan.pa.rgyas.byed m.
Kun.mthun.dge.legs m.
Rgud.pa.las.rgyal m.
Ma.ruṅ.bdud.ḥdul m.
Sku.tshe.sriṅs.byed m.
Sri.gcod.sri.gnon m.
Ri.gnon.ri.ḥdul m.
Ṅan.sbyoṅ.yaṅ.ḥdul m.
Phyogs.las.rnam.rgyal m.
Ḥdzam.gliṅ.mthaḥ.brtan mchod.sdoṅ
Lo.kun.mthun.paḥi m.
Hbyuṅ.ba.kun.mthun m.
Byuṅ.ba.cha.sñoms m.
Bkra.śis.brtsegs.paḥi m.
Rtsa.ba.stobs.chen m.

Stūpas

Stūpas

Stūpas were erected as objects of worship during the lifetime of the Buddha. He gave eight handfuls of his hair by stroking his head, to Trapuṣa and Bhallika. He further instructed them on how to configure a *stūpa*. They returned to their home in Bactria and erected a *stūpa* at Asitañjana. It is mentioned by Hsiian-tsang. A *stūpa* is built after taking compassion for all creatures as the guiding principle, and the thought of Enlightenment *(bodhicitta)* as the base, so says the *Diamond Light Dhāraṇī*. The *stūpa* is a symbol to induce good thoughts in people to do good deeds *(puṇya)*.

Eight *stūpas* represent the major events in the Buddha's life. There is an erroneous concept that *stūpas* are funerary monuments. The eight *stūpas* celebrate the Buddha's birth at Lumbinī, the Enlightenment at Vajrāsana, the grand miracle at Śrāvastī, the first sermon at Sarnath, the submission of the elephant at Rājagṛha, the descent from Trayastriṁśa heaven at Sāṅkāśya, the offering of honey by the monkey at Vaiśālī, and his *Mahāparinirvāṇa* at Kuśīnagara. There are divergences in the enumeration of events, their localities as well as their builders.

The Eight *Nirvāṇa-stūpas* were constructed on the physical relics of the Buddha by eight kings who were lay persons, as distinguished from the monkhood. There are also commemorative *stūpas* built to remember some special event for spiritual well-being. A *sūtra* lays two preconditions for the building of a *stūpa*: 'compassion for all creatures as the guiding principle, and the thought of illumination as the base.'

The *stūpa* on pg. 189 is the fourth in the foregoing series, representing Perfect Enlightenment. In the rotund cupola is the letter *'HRĪ'* out of which stream forth rays of light purifying the sins and ignorance of all that lives, after their attachments are ended and all *Dharmas* have become empty.

Svayambhunāth

The Dharmadhātu Stūpa at Svayambhunāth—the Self-Existent Lord—has played a prominent role in the Buddhist world, ever since its foundation about the beginning of the 5th century by King Vṛṣadeva. It was a prime object of worship in Licchavī Nepal. The *stūpa* is also known by its Newari name Sinagu, Syengu or other variants. It is one of the four *stūpas* set up by Vṛṣadeva and his successors to sanctify the four quarters. Among the myriad cult sites in the Kathmandu Valley, Svayambhu is the most sacred. The *Svayambhū-purāṇa* narrates its miraculous nature. Svayambhū chose to manifest himself in the midst of Kālīhrada or Nāgavāsa, the lake that filled the Valley before

FACING PAGE: *Svayambhunath is the ontological source of the sacred environs of the Kathmandu Valley. Its myth figures prominently in the* Svayambhū-purāṇa. *Svayambhunath is the earthly manifestation of Mount Meru.*

man, or even Paśupati, dwelt therein. A flame, or alternately an image of crystal 'one cubit high,' Svayambhu-in-the-form-of-light *(Jyotīrūpa)* emanated from a resplendent lotus as large as the wheel of a chariot. It had ten thousand golden petals. It had diamonds above, pearls below, and rubies in the middle. Its pollen consisted of jewels. Its seed lobes were gold, and stalks lapis lazuli. In time, however, the compassionate Bodhisattva Mañjuśrī, finding the lake 'full of monstrous aquatic animals and the temple of Svayambhu almost inaccessible, opened with his sword the valley' and drained the lake. Then the Bodhisattva Vajrasattva 'fearing that wicked men in the Kaliyuga would steal away the jewels of Svayambhu and destroy his image, concealed him under a slab of stone.'

Bodhnāth

The Bodhnāth Stūpa, called Bya-ruṅ-kha-śor in Tibetan, is the second of the famous landmarks of Kathmandu, the capital of Nepal. Situated on the main trade route of Tibet it is considered one of the holy of the holies of Lamaism. Surmounted by a large white dome, its Eyes of Compassion, symbolising the Eleven-headed Avalokiteśvara, cast their grace on the valley and on the visiting devotees who circumambulate it, turning the prayer wheels. The thirteen diminishing segments of its spire symbolise either the thirteen heavens,

ABOVE: *Bodhnath Stūpa founded by a Licchavi king in the sixth century. Tibetans enclosed the old ruined Licchavi Stūpa within the grand construction that it is today. Its elaborate plinth emulates the Gyantse Stūpa in Western Tibet.*

or better, the ten unique powers *(daśa-bala)* of the Buddha and the three special applications of awareness *(āveṇika-smṛti-upasthāna)* according to the Tibetan Tanjur.

According to Nepalese chronicles, Bodhnāth was built around AD 500 by King Manadeva of the Licchavī Dynasty.

Tsoṅ-kha-pa and Sitātapatrā are shown near the top of the *stūpa*, followed by the Panchen and Dalai Lamas and the White and Green Tārās in the second row. At the *stūpa* are the Eight Auspicious Emblems of the umbrella, fish, vase, lotus in the first row, and the conch, endless knot *(śrīvatsa)*, victorious banner and wheel. The umbrella *(chattra)* symbolises the universal impirium of *Dharma*; fish *(matsya)*, the freedom of the perfectly emancipated; vase *(kalaśa)*, affluence; and lotus, purity amidst the sullied *saṁsāra*. The conch *(śaṅkha)* is symbolic of the sacred word; the endless knot *(śrīvatsa)* of love, devotion and longevity; the victorious banner, attainment of Enlightenment; and the wheel *(Dharmacakra)* represents *Dharma* set in motion.

Below the original woodprint, the traditional Lamaist account of its origin is narrated. Being questioned by King Khri-sroṅ-ldeḥu-btsan, Padmasambhava told him that in times of yore, Avalokiteśvara vowed to save beings from the vortex of *samsar*ic existence.

ABOVE: *The fourth of the 8 Stūpas, it represents the Enlightenment of Śākyamuni Buddha.*

Guardian Deities

The Four Lokapālas

The four directions are guarded by the four *lokapālas*, also known as the Caturmahārājika or the Four Great Kings (Tibetan: Rgyal-chen bzhi). They are mentioned in the earliest Buddhist works as attending on the Buddha while yet in the Tuṣita Heaven, and who assisted at his birth, held aloft the hoofs of his horse Kanthaka when he left the palace for the forest, and were present at his *nirvāṇa*.

Dhṛtarāṣṭra

Dhṛtarāṣṭra (right) guards the east and rules over the *gandharvas* and *piśācas*. He plays a stringed *vīṇā*, his distinctive mark. White in colour, he is clad in full armour, with high North Asian boots and a high helmet. He is shown standing as well as sitting on a skin.

Virūpākṣa

Virūpāksa (facing page) holds a *stūpa* in his left hand and is girdled by a serpent *(nāga)*. He is the guardian of the west. His body colour is red and the dress is of a warrior clad in armour, breastplate, backpiece, bellypiece and strong boots, with a flowing *dhotī*.

Vaiśravaṇa

Vaiśravaṇa's (pgs. 194, 195) body, like pure gold, is yellow, radiating with the brilliance of

FACING PAGE: *Virūpākṣa is the guardian of the west and his metropolis is Bhogavatī.*

ABOVE: *Dhṛtarāṣṭra the* Lokapāla *of the East, with his distinctive attribute, the* vīṇā.

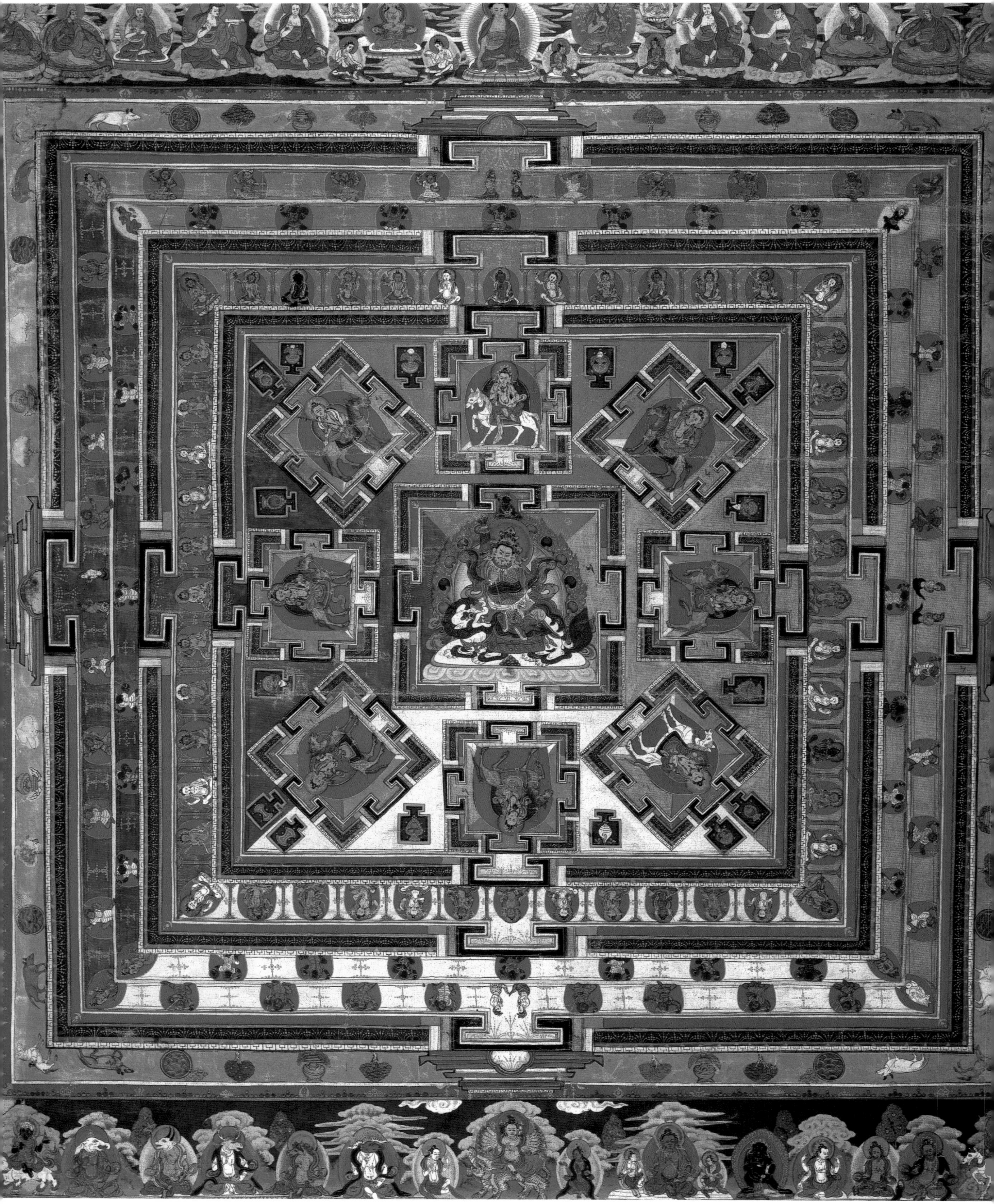

ABOVE AND FACING PAGE: *Vaiśravaṇa with his eight great* yakṣa *generals on horses. His cult centres around health and longevity. He cures physical illness and dispels spiritual confusion. His Paradise of Pure Emerald in the east rivals the wonders of the Western Paradise of Sukhāvatī.*

Dhṛtarāṣṭra (east)

Virūpākṣa (west)

a hundred thousand rising suns. In his right hand he holds a banner of victory adorned with the wish-granting jewel, and in his left hand rests the treasure-producing mongoose. In keeping with his position as a dispenser of wealth, he is richly dressed in flowing garments of silk and wears a diadem and ornaments of gold. On his right shoulder rests the disk of the sun, and on the left shoulder the moon. He rides on a white lion.

On the top is Vajrapāṇi. Vaiśravaṇa is surrounded by the Eight Marshals. Richly attired, all of them hold the treasure-producing mongoose in their left hand. They can be distinguished by the colour of their bodies and by the attributes in their right hands.

Vaiśravaṇa has two predominant functions: one as the dispenser of riches; the God of Wealth, as a *nidhipati.* His second role is that of the king of *yakṣa*s, and as one of the four directions, he rules over the north. According to the *Suvarṇabhāsa-sutra* and other texts, the Four *Lokapāla*s defend the four points of the compass against evil and protect the faithful from all odds.

Vaiśravaṇa is represented seated on a lion in his mystic circle *(cakra),* holding the banner of victory in his right hand and a treasure-emitting mongoose in the left. Jewels flow forth from the mouth of the mongoose in abundance and spread over the entire woodcut. In the centre of the body of Vaiśravaṇa is the mystic circle with six concentric

ABOVE AND FACING PAGE: *The four* lokapāla*s or four* mahārājika*s protect their respective kingdoms in the east, south, west and north on the four sides of Mount Sumeru. They appear in the second century* BC *on the railings of Barhut and in the first century* BC *on the gates of Sanchi.*

circles surrounded by a seventh circle of flames. The concentric circles start from the innermost which has a *vajra* with the *mantra*. In the next circle is the Tibetan prayer that the mystic circle of Vaiśravaṇa with all his retinue may be firmly established so that wealth, happiness and prosperity may increase. The third circle comprises eight leaves of the lotus containing invocations to the Eight Marshals.

Virūḍhaka

Virūḍhaka (bottom right) He guards the south, and holds a sword in his right hand, whose edge he touches with his left hand. He is blue in colour, sits on a bull and wears the elephant helmet. He is wrathful, and wears an armour and a flying scarf.

Beg-tse

Chief defender of *Dharma* in the retinue of Vajrabhairava is Beg-tse (pgs. 198, 199), also known as Lcam-sriṅ (brother-and-sister), who is represented with a copper cuirass and brandishing a blazing sword. Though fiendish in appearance, he has only two arms. His left hand carries to his mouth the heart of those who break vows and under it he clasps a bow and arrow. He is red in colour, has three eyes and a crown of skulls on his head, and a girdle of heads on his waist. According to a liturgy by the Panchen Lama Blo-bzaṅ-dpal-ldan Bstan-paḥi-ñi-

Vaiśravaṇa (north)

Virūḍhaka (south)

ABOVE AND FACING PAGE: *The four* lokapālas *are also represented in scenes of the Buddha's life as offering four bowls to Śākyamuni to break his fast. In Central Asia they were transformed into warriors clad in armour and breast-plate. In the* Saṁyuktāgama *the Buddha summons them to his couch and enjoins them to defend the* Dharma *in evil times.*

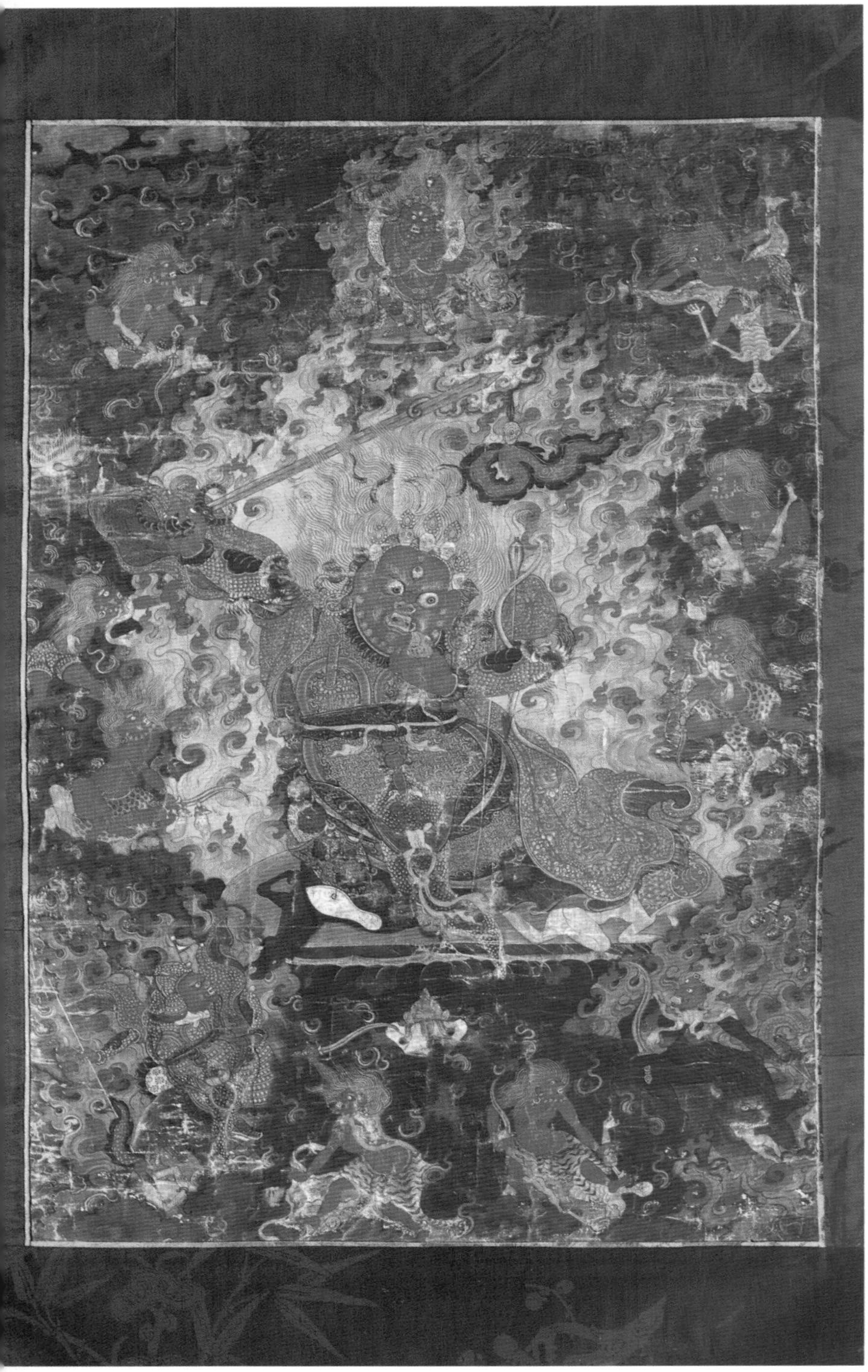

ma, his task is to destroy and exterminate all those who offend the teachings of the Buddha. Like the other indigenous terrific deities, he was received into the Lamaist pantheon as a custodian of temples and sacred things, and above all as a watchful defender of the faith. He ruthlessly punishes those who break their vows or offend the sanctity of *Dharma*. He is a btsan or native deity and custodian of temples as well as protector of the Gelukpas.

On his left stands his sister, Beg-tse. She is riding on a lioness, which tramples a human body.

Beg-tse and his sister Vidyādevī cannot be separated which is why they are known as Lcam-sriṅ—brother-and-sister. He is red in colour, because of his abode in the copper mountain. His right arm wields a copper sword to slay anyone who breaks his vows, and the left carries the hearts of enemies. Originally a Mongolian war-god, he was transformed into a defender of the faith. He became a *Yidam* of the Gelukpas in celebration of the penetration of their denomination of Buddhism among the Mongolians. The right foot of Beg-tse crushes a horse and the left tramples a human corpse.

Assimilation of local deities of Tibet into the Buddhist pantheon enriched the visual attraction of the ever-conquering energy. They became protective deities or *Dharmapālas*. For instance, Dpal-ldan Lha-mo became the chief guardian-goddess of the Gelukpa School and Ma-gcig

ABOVE AND FACING PAGE: *Beg-tse means 'hidden coat of mail.' A protective deity, he tried to obstruct the journey of Dalai Lama Bsod-nams-rgya-mtsho to Mongolia in 1575 but was defeated and came to be worshipped as a* Dharmapāla.

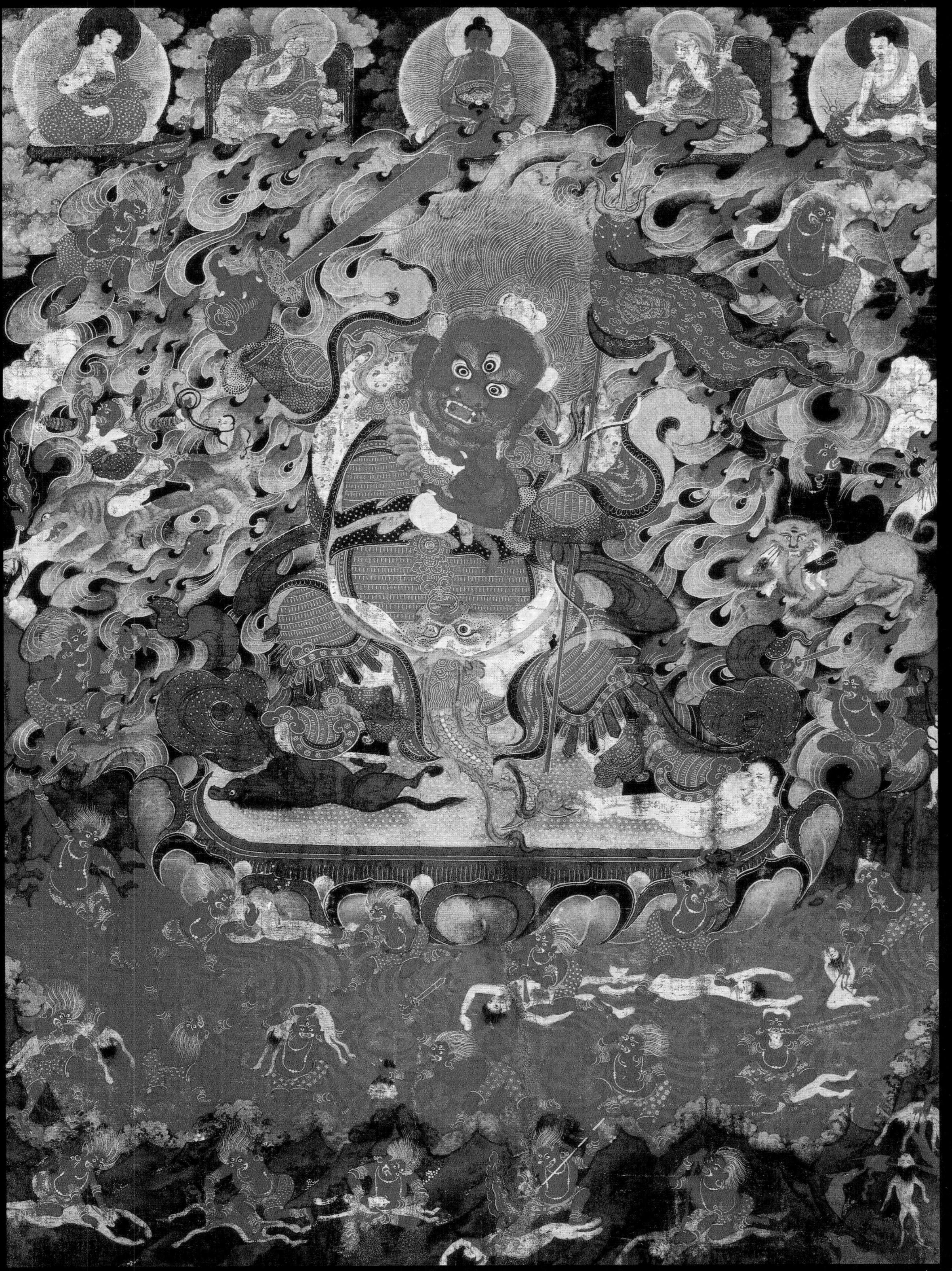

Dpal-ldan Lha-mo was considered the principal protectress of the Tibetan capital Lhasa.

Red Tsiḥu

He emerges from the exuberant profusion of the pre-Buddhist mythic world of Tibet, as the guardian of the Samye Monastery. As leader of the *tsan* demons, he became the guardian of the first Buddhist monastery of Tibet, founded by Padmasambhava in the 8th century by the favour of King Khri Sroṅ-lde-btsan, as a pageant of the Buddhist cosmos with 108 chapels, around which the universe unrolls and revolves. His forehead is contorted in anger. His upper teeth gnaws the lower lip. He brandishes a banner of red silk in the right hand and in his left hand he holds the snare of the *tsan* demons which he throws with the speed of lightning on enemies, catching with it their 'life-breath'. On his right side he carries a quiver of tiger-skin and on his left side a bow-case made from the skin of a leopard; he rides a black horse. On his head he wears a helmet of leather, adorned with an aigrette of vulture-feathers. His consort is Lha-mo Hrol-mo spyan-gcig-ma. She is dark brown, naked, has one face, and her two hands hold a chopper and a snare. A single eye stares in a fierce manner from the middle of her brow.

Red Tsiḥu resides at Samye in a building where the ancient mask known as the srid-paḥi smug-chuṅ is preserved. The outer walls of the edifice are covered with red cloth. He is expected to exterminate enemies.

Five Protective Kings of Tibet (Sku-lṅa)

Pe-har (pgs. 203, 204) is in the centre of the Five Kings. He occupies a foremost position among the Gelukpas. He has different names depending upon his functions. The original home of Pe-har has given rise to a vast legendary literature whose bewildering details preserve various traditions about his introduction into the Tibetan pantheon. According to one tradition, he came from Za-Hor in Bengal, while another alleges that he left Za-Hor and went to Bhata-Hor in the Uigur country where he was the tutelary deity of the Hor tribes. Padmasambhava appointed him as a guardian of the treasures of the Samye Monastery. He stayed at Samye for seven centuries, and eventually moved to his present residence at the Nechung Monastery near Drepung under the reign of the Fifth Dalai Lama Ṅag-dbaṅ-blo-bzaṅ-rgya-mtsho (1617–1682). He is the State Oracle at Nechung.

The Sku-lṅa or Five Protective Kings of Tibet, wear a broad-rimmed cane-hat with Pe-har

FACING PAGE: *Red Tsiḥu is invoked to exterminate enemies:*
Together with your hordes, come surging forward,
Soar quickly atop the enemies.
With the flaming iron hook, tear out their heart-veins;
Having chewed the bodies of the foes with your flaming teeth,
Swallow them down into your stomach which is like a *rākṣasa*-hole.

presiding in the centre. The other four facing the four directions have flowing red robes with green hems.

Pe-har is white, and rides a white lion. He has three eyes and three faces which are white, sky-blue and red, and six arms. The three right hands hold an iron hook, arrow and sword, while the three left ones have a knife, bow and sack. He wears a tiger-skin as loin-cloth, resides in the north in a blue palace of turquoise, and emanates from the sacred syllable '*TRI*' as he is three-faced. He is the king of the *karma* plane. On top of the painting are Atiśa, Tsoṅ-kha-pa and Padmasambhava who forced the Five Kings to make a vow to be guardians of the first Buddhist monastery, Samye. At the bottom are the offerings of the five senses, represented by the following organs: two eyes, a heart flanked by two ears, a nose and a tongue in a cranium.

On the facing page is an exquisitely painted scroll of the Five Protective Kings of Tibet. Their placement is as follows: 1. Pe-har, 2. Brgya-byin, 3. Mon-bu-pu-ta, 4. Śiṅ-bya-can, 5. Dgra-lha skyes-gcig-bu. All of them are without their consorts.

4 Śiṅ-bya-can		5 Dgra-lha skyes-gcig-bu
	1 Pe-har	
3 Mon-bu-pu-ta		2 Brgya-byin

The symbolism of the various attributes of Pe-har is as follows: 'As a sign of keeping your oath, you hold a thunderbolt; as a *Yidam*-token you hold a rosary of crystal, and as an *abhiṣeka*-sign you carry a *phur-bu* of iron; come to this place, great *Dharmarāja*. As the sign of a warlord you brandish a "banner of victory" with a tiger's head on top; as a token of Bodhisattvahood you lift a stick and a vessel; as a token of your position as a *Dharmapāla* you wear a hat and high boots. Come to this place, you, the Dkor-sruṅ rgyal-po. To express your peaceful mood you show a smiling face; a sign of your fierce nature are the bloodshot eyes; a sign of your wrathful mood is the ferocious "Ha, Ha" laughter; you, the Great Fierce One, come to this place. In order to guard the religious precepts, you ride on a white lion. To subdue the enemies and obstacle-creating demons you ride on an elephant with a long trunk; in order to carry out magic actions, you mount a three-legged mule, come and partake of the offerings, presented to you!'

Local Protective Deity

The scroll on page 205 is that of a local protective deity, who belongs to the category of Ḥjig-rten-

FACING PAGE: *In the past Pe-har resided in the blue sky and he was Tshaṅs-pa or Brahmā, the Ruler of the Thirty-three Gods. In the middle* kalpa *he dwelt in the country of Hor where he presided over the meditation school. Finally, he took his residence at Samye Monastery, from where he ruled over entire Tibet.*

paḥi-sruṅ-ma or local guardians. As such they are of importance only for a particular place or monastery and are too many to be counted. He wears a broad-rimmed hat worn by deities of the royal class. His right hand bears jewels and the left hand, a lance with a flag. The jewel held in the right hand is a characteristic attribute of protectors of religion who are believed to be owners of treasures. A long lance is also carried by protectors of religion. The red lance and the spotted banner are their characteristic weapons. The *Dharmapālas* protect *Dharma,* its institutions, its 'Land of Snows' against all kinds of adversaries. They crush human and supernatural enemies of Buddhism, and are hence of fierce aspect.

Nāgarāja

Nāgas are one of the eight classes of beings: *deva* (god), *nāga, yakṣa, gandharva, asura* (demon), *garuḍa, kinnara* and *mahoraga*. Mythic beings with bodies ending in serpentine tails, they live in springs, rivers and deep in the oceanic underworld. They were entrusted by the Buddha to preserve the books of transcendental wisdom, the *Prajñā-pāramitā,* until such a time that the human race could comprehend and transmit them. It was the great Buddhist teacher Nāgārjuna who received the *Prajñā-pāramitā* from the *nāgas* and promulgated

ABOVE: *A local protective deity.*

FACING PAGE: *Pe-har stayed at Samye for seven centuries, and during the reign of the Fifth Dalai Lama (AD 1617-1682) he moved to the Nechung Monastery near the Drepung Monastery. There are several conflicting accounts about him.*

its doctrines. In the early representation, *nāga*s had human form with three, five or seven snake-hoods coiling out behind their head. After the 12th century, their body shapes tapered into a serpentine tail. Eight *nāga*s with seven hoods are mentioned in the *Niṣpanna-yogāvalī:* Ananta, Vāsuki, Takṣaka, Karkoṭaka, Padma, Mahāpadma, Śāṅkhapāla and Kulika.

*Nāgarāja*s are benevolent when propitiated and protect from lightning, stop floods or bring beneficial showers. A *nāgarāja* (facing page) with a vase of ambrosia in his hands is invoked to prolong life.

Weather-making is an important ritual in the cultural space of Tibetan Buddhism. *Nāga*s who dwell in water are said to withhold rain if offended by the sinful actions of men. Hundreds of *nāga*s are found in Bon works. Buddhists have adopted them in their weather-making rites. These old traditions were modified at the time of Tsoṅ-kha-pa and the ceremonies came to centre around Varuṇa and his companions. He is known as Klu-rgyal Varuṇa—Varuṇa, the King of *Nāga*s, or Apalāla the Prince Terrible.

FACING PAGE: *One of the four Nāgarāja scrolls. They had different colours of the body: green, red, light vermilion and blue. Here the nāgarāja is light vermilion in colour, and dwells in the ocean. The worship of* nāgas *was an important part of Buddhism.* Nāgas *became an object of a complicated liturgy that conformed to the cults of the klu of the Bons.*

Conclusion

With the majority of the monasteries and monks, scrolls and statues desecrated and lost in Tibet, the agony of their absence begs the question of the future of this glorious art. It is a hymn of multiple expressions of Life as it seeks the bread of its Being. Even today, in the very heart of Beijing stands the Lamaist monastery of Yung-ho-kung which has a colossal image of Maitreya, 23 metres high, carved from the trunk of a white sandalwood tree which took ten years to transport from Tibet. Emperor Ch'ien-lung had conceived it 'as the Buddha's Jetavana Park, adorning it with the beauty of religious paintings, perfuming it with incense, holding services with morning chants and evening bells ... your great bounty will flow harmoniously' (this long inscription dated December 1774 is a masterpiece of poetic diction). Thousands of young boys and girls pray everyday at this most important temple in Beijing to seek blessings and to savour the flavour of all-enveloping love and august grace. In India itself, a large Tibetan community has created gorgeous monasteries with *thaṅka*s, images, scriptures that have become repositories of all the aspects of Tibetan Buddhism, from in-depth studies to the ritual of logical debates. *Thaṅka* painting, Tibetan medicine, astrology and astronomy preserve a holistic panorama. Sikkim, Ladakh, Lahul and Spiti have very ancient monasteries where the tradition lives in the loneliness of barren rocks. Bhutan is an outstanding Vajrāyana country where all the radiations and shapes can be seen and meditated upon, as has been the case for more than a thousand years. The Mongolian People's Republic is the second Vajrāyana country where for the last sixteen years, monastery building has recorded a boom. After the wounded years of Communist cultural genocide, spring has now returned. In the new dispensation, years of light have dawned in Mongolia. As a Mongolian professor said to me in 1991: 'I am light to eyes long blind.' The Mongols of Inner Mongolia in China, and of Buryatia as well as Kalmykia in the Russian Federation are busy restoring their sublime centuries, as they seek the culmination of their dreams among the stones of desecration.

*Thaṅka*s, scrolls, statues, *sramaṇa*s and *sutra*s are the collective consciousness *(ālaya-vijñāna)* where Lamaism has its deep roots. Links with the land, with the past and with their identity were the bonds between the realms of reality and possibility. Man is always standing in front of himself seeking active fragments of his interior life. They are projections of his innermost individuality, the shadow of his thoughts. *Maṇḍala*s, fierce deities like Mahākāla, the constantly changing patterns, are to purify the images of fantasy by esoteric knowledge. In Tibet, *yogis* are devoted to the practice of Gcod—'cutting off' the cosmic illusion. The surges, throbs and quickening rhythms of universal energy are the mighty breath that holds the key of life and death.

When the hardware of galloping modern technology has completed the eco-grazing of our planet and humanity stands groping for direction, seeking a quantum jump towards wholeness, then the tiny pebbles of the spirit gathered on the shoreline of life will become fine pearls, which we will carry back to our hearts, intertwined with the Sea of Conciousness. *Thaṅkas* are the symbols of a creative harmony beyond the contemporary mad rush of *Homo economicus*. Cosmic humanism is God in the image of Man. In the words of J.R. Oppenheimer: 'Always in the past there has been an explanation of immense sweep and simplicity ... Do we even have confidence that we shall have the wit to discover it.' Ma-gcig Lab-sgron-ma practised zhi-byed—the difficult art of checking passions and realising the insubstantiality of things. Will inordinate greed destroy the human race? Perhaps.

Thaṅkas are the wholeness of value systems with humans, nature and transcendence waking the worlds with a lion's roar. Let us remember the words of Hegel: 'Beware the cunning of reason.' A wandering *yoginī* says to Siddha Kantali:

Envision the rags you pick and stitch as empty space.
See your needle as mindfulness and knowledge.
Thread this needle with compassion
And stitch new clothing for all the sentient beings
of the three realms.

Glossary

Abhidharma	Buddhist philosophy and psychology
abhaya	fearlessness
abhaya mudrā	hand gesture of fearlessness
Abhidharma-kośa	exhaustive study of the *Sarvāstivāda abhidharma*
Abhisamayālaṅkāra	analysis of the *prajñā-pāramitā* doctrines
abhiṣeka	consecration
abhyucca	colossal
ādarśa-jñāna	mirror-like knowledge
ādhāra	fundament
Advayavajra-saṅgraha	collection of the writings of Advayavajra
akṣara	syllable
Akṣobhya-vyūha	text on Akṣobhya's paradise
ālaya-vijñāna	collective consciousness
ālīḍha	attitude in which the right knee is advanced and the left leg drawn back
amāvasyā	the night of new moon
amogha	unfailing
amṛta	nectar
amṛta-kalaśa	vase of nectar
amūrta	unmanifest
ananta	infinite
anantābha	Infinite Light
Ananta-prabha	Infinite Effulgence
añjali	folded hands
añjali-mudrā	*mudrā* of folded hands
antaka	destroyer
Anuttara Yoga	Supreme yoga
arjuna	white
arapacana mantra	mantra of the five syllables *a ra pa ca na*
arura	myrobalan
asura	demon
Atiyoga	a higher form of yoga
ātman	soul
Avataṁsaka	a class of Buddhist *sūtras*
āveṇika-smṛti-upasthāna	special applications of awareness, threefold reticence
bali-vidhi	ritual of offerings
bīja	hieronym or sacred syllable as the abbreviated name of the deity
bimba	image
bodhi	Enlightenment
bhūmi	planes (of *dhyāna,* etc.)
Bhadrakalpa	the present aeon
Bhadra-kalpika Sūtra	the Sutra of the Thousand Buddhas of our aeon
bhadrāsana	posture of sitting with the legs hanging down in European fashion
bhūmi-sparśa mudrā	*mudrā* of touching the Earth (Goddess as a witness)
bodhicitta	the mind or will to attain Enlightenment
Bodhyagrī mudrā	the *mudrā* of Supreme Enlightenment
caitya	*stupa*
cakra	wheel
cakravartin	Universal Emperor
campaka	*Michelia campaka,* a yellow fragrant flower
caṇḍa	fierce
caṇḍī	inner heat generated by yogic process
caturmahārājika	Four Guardians of the World

Caṇḍa-mahāroṣaṇa	name of a ferocious deity
cintāmaṇi	wish-granting jewel
citta	mind
Citra-lakṣaṇa	name of text on iconography
chattra	parasol
Ḍāka	imp-like beings
Ḍākinī	female imp
ḍamaru	drum
dāna	donation
dāna-pāramitā	Perfection of Giving, one of the six perfections (*pāramitās*)
daśa-bala	ten powers, one who possesses the ten *balas*, used as a synonym of tathāgata
dehe viśvasya ānanam	the consubstantiation of the universe and the body. The body is microtheos
deva	deity
Dharma	the Buddhist faith, doctrine, spirituality
Dharmacakra	Wheel of Law
Dharmacakra-mudrā	*mudrā* of turning the Wheel of Law
Dharmadhātu	the universe of the Absolute
Dharma-kāya	spiritual body
Dharmarāja	Yama the God of Death
Dharmatā-jñāna	knowledge of the norm
dhāraṇī	invocation for special effectiveness
dhotī	lower garment
dhyāna-mudrā	*mudrā* of meditation
dhyāna-pāramitā	Perfection of Meditation. One of the six *pāramitās*
dikpāla	gods of the (ten) directions
durgati-pariśodhana	purification of evil destinies
dūrvā	panicum grass
gandha	fragrance
Gaṇḍavyūha	name of the final *sutra* of the Avataṁsaka category
gaṇḍī	bell
gandharva	a class of beings
garuḍa	a mythical bird
Gsaṅ-sñiṅ	name of an esoteric text 'Esoteric Heart'
Guhyasamāja	title of a *tantra*
Guhyasamāja Tantra	title of a *tantra*
Guru Yoga	meditation on the Guru as a Deity
halāhala	a kind of deadly poison
Haṭha Yoga	yoga of physical exercises
ḥdre	goblin, evil spirit
iṣṭadevatā	tutelary deity
jātaka	stories of the former births of the Buddha
jaya	victory
Jyotīrūpa	light-form
kalaśa	vase
kāma	passion
kamaṇḍalu	gourd-vessel
Kanjur	collection of over 1100 *sutras* as the Canon in 108 volumes
kapāla	cranium, skull
Kapāladhara	one who holds crania
karma	ritual
karma-kalaśa	ritual vase
kartrī	chopper
karuṇā	compassion
kāya	body
khakkhara	monk's staff
khaṭvāṅga	skull-topped staff
kinnara	a class of beings
kiśorī	adolescent girl

kṣānti-pāramitā	the perfection of intellectual receptivity
kumbhāṇḍa	a class of beings
lalita	charming, lovely
lalitāsana	posture of relaxation
laukika	worldly, mundane
loka	world
lokottara	transcendental, supramundane
Mādhyamika	a system of Buddhist philosophy, the Middle Way
Madhyamaka-kārikā	basic text of Mādhyamika philosophy
mahāsukha	supreme bliss
maitrī	benevolence towards all beings that is free from attachment
Mahāmudrā	the highest teaching of Vajrayāna: realisation of emptiness, freedom from *samsara* and their inseperability
Mahāparinirvāṇa	supreme *nirvāṇa*
Mahāvyutpatti	title of Sanskrit Tibetan lexicon of Buddhist terminology
mahoraga	a class of beings
makara	sea monster
maṇi	jewel
Maṇi Kambum	a work on early Tibetan history
maṇḍala	cosmogram or symbolic representation of the sanctum of a deity for meditation
mantra	power-laden invocation for meditation
Mañju	charming
Māra	Evil One, Satan
matsya	fish
māyā	phenomenal world of forms, in opposition to the immutable absolute
Māyājāla	name of a *tantra* text
mleccha	heathen
mudrā	hand gesture
mūrti	image
Na adevo devam arcayet	one who has not divinised himself should not adore the divine
nāḍī	energy channels through *prāṇa* passes
nāga	serpent, a class of beings
nāgakesara	blossom of *Mesua roxburghii*
Nāgarāja	King of *Nāga*s
Naimittika	accidental (opposite to eternal)
nakula	mongoose
nakulaka	purse made by stitching the skin of a mongoose
namaskāra-mudrā	*mudrā* of salutation
Nandimitra-avadāna	the legends of the Sixteen Apostles of the Buddha, written by Nandimitra
nidhipati	lord of treasures
nimitta	occasion, cause
nirākāra	aniconic
nirmāṇa-kāya	one of the three *kāya*s. Representation as a monk.
Nirvāṇa	emancipation
Nirvāṇa-stūpa	the *stupa* of the *nirvāṇa* of the Buddha
Niṣpanna-yogāvalī	Abhayākaragupta's handbook of *maṇḍala*s
pañca	five
Pañcakrama	name of a text
pañca-raśmi	five scintillations
pāramitā	perfection. There are usually six perfections
pāśa	noose
patasha	sugar-pie
piśāca	a class of demons
piṭakadhara	one who has mastered the Buddhist Canon
phur-bu	ritual dagger
pothi	Indian style open-leaf book
prajñā	wisdom
prajñā-khaḍga	sword of wisdom

Prajñā-pāramitā	perfection of wisdom, one of the six perfections
Pramāṇa-samuccaya	a text on logic
Pramāṇa-vārttika	a text on logic
prāṇāyāma	breathing exercises
pratyekabuddha	an Enlightened One who has attained Enlightenment for himself
pratyavekṣanā-jñāna	knowledge through reflection
puṇya	merit
pūrṇimā	full moon
rāga	passion
rāga-raktā	vehement in passion
rākṣasa	demon
Ratnakūṭa	a genre of Buddhist Sūtras
rūpaṁ śūnyatā	form is the void
ṣaḍ-akṣara	six-syllabled
ṣaḍ-gati	birth as six kinds of beings
sādhaka	visualiser
sādhana	visualisation
Sādhanamālā	a major text on the visualisation of Buddhist deities
sahaja	innate
sahasrāra	thousand-spoked
sahasra-vīra	with thousands of heroes
sākāra	iconic
samādhi	a state of non-dualistic consciouness
samādhi-mudrā	*mudrā* of *samādhi*
śamatha	calming the mind to attain *vipaśyanā* or insight into the true nature of *śūnyatā*
samatā-jñāna	knowledge of equanimity
samaya	vow
samaya-maṇḍala	*maṇḍala* with symbolic forms of deities in place of the anthropomorphic
sambodhi	full Enlightenment
sambhoga-kāya	body of delight, *i.e.*, representation with crown and royal ornaments
saṁsāra	cycle of existences
Samyak-Sambuddha	perfectly enlightened
saṁskāra	empirical impulses
śaṅkha	conch
śastra	weapon
siddha	tantric masters
Siddhānta	doctrinal views
siddhi	mastery over the powers of the body and of nature
śīla-pāramitā	perfection of discipline, one of the six *pāramitā*s
sramaṇa	monk
śrīvatsa	endless knot: an attribute of deities
śṛṅgāra rasa	erotic sentiment
strī-ratna	jewel of a woman
stūpa	a focal structure in Buddhist monasteries as a cult centre
Sukhāvatī-vyūha	a text on Sukhāvatī, the Western Paradise of Amitābha
śūla	spike
Sumeru	cosmic mountain at the centre of the world
śūnya	void
śūnyatā eva rūpam	The void is form
suparṇa	the mythical bird garuḍa
sūtra	a Buddhist sacred text
svatantra	one of the two schools of Mādhyamika philosophy
Svayambhū-purāṇa	name of a text on the Buddhist holy places in Nepal
svayambhū-rūpa	self-existent form
Tantra	esoteric Buddhism or texts thereof
thaṅka	painting on a flat surface
Tārā	a Buddhist goddess
tarjanī-mudrā	the *mudrā* of threatening

tārayati	leads across (The Ocean of Existence)
tridaṇḍī	three-forked staff
trikāya	three bodies: *dharma-kāya, sambhoga-kāya, nirmāṇa-kāya*
utpala	blue lotus
upāya	skillful means or method
upāya-kauśalya	conspicuous ability in skillful means
uṣṇīṣa	fillet, excrescence on the head of the Buddha
Uṣṇīṣavijayā-dhāraṇī	a text to invoke Uṣṇīṣavijayā the Goddess of Supreme Victory
vaiḍūrya	beryl
vajra	diamond as a symbol of the indestructible
vajra-hūṁkāra mudrā	*mudrā* of the symbol *hūṁkāra*
vajra-katarī	scissor with a vajra-handle
vajra-paryaṅka	a seating position
vajra-pāśa	noose with a handle of vajra
vajrāsana	a seating position
vajrasattva	Diamond Being: the symbol of purity and spiriual purification
Vajrāvalī	a text on Vajrayāna ritual
vāk	speech, one of the three esoteric categories *(kāya, vāk, citta)*
vāmana	dwarf
vasu	wealth
varada	giving boons
varada-mudrā	*mudrā* of giving boons
vijaya-kalaśa	victory vase
vighna	hindrances
vijñāna	consciousness
Vijñānavāda	Conscious-only school of Mahāyāna philosophy
Vijñaptimātratā	*siddhi:* a work on ten Yogācāra masters, a complete compendium of the system
vīṇā	Indian lute
Vinaya	Book of Buddhist Monastic Discipline
vipaśyanā	analytical examination of the nature of things leads to insight
viśvapadma	multi-petalled lotus
viśva-vajra	crossed *vajra*
vitarka-mudrā	*mudrā* of disputation
virya-pāramitā	perfection of exertion, one of the six *pāramitā*s
Viṣṇu-sahasra-nāma	a hymn of the thousand epithets of Viṣṇu
Yab-Yum	'Father and Mother' or the Deity in embrace with his consort
yakṣa	a class of beings
Yama	God of Death
Yidam	tutelary deity
yoga	seeking union with the Divine
Yogācāra	a school of Buddhism in which the central notion is 'mind only'
Yogācāra-bhūmi-śāstra	a comprehensive text of Yogācāra philosophy
yoga-paṭṭa	a band tied to maintain a yogic posture for a long time
Yogin	one who practises *yoga*
yoginī	a lady *yogin*
Yoginī Niguma	the consort of Padmasambhava

Acknowledgements

The major part of the *thaṅkas* in this book come from the collection of my father, the late Prof. RaghuVira, who made extensive trips to several Buddhist countries in Asia. Others are from the Museum of Fine Arts, Bogd-khan Palace Museum and the personal collection of the artist Tsultem: all from Ultaanbaatar, the capital of the Mongolian People's Republic.

Some originate from private collections in Basel, Zurich, Switzerland. A few are from the Schoettle Collection in Munich, besides one each from Sergej Diakoff, Heinrich Harrer, Museum of Local Studies at Ulanude (Buryatia, Russian Federation), Musée Guimet, Paris and the Ethnographical Museum of Stockholm.

I thank them for conserving these treasures of incandescent inner experiences, with gods mighty, luminous and serene; in a truly independent artistic idiom created by the supreme culture of the 'Land of Snows.'

Tibetan Art has been possible due to the enthusiastic initiative of Mr Bikash D. Niyogi and Mrs Tultul D. Niyogi who have taken a continuing interest in taking *Tibetan Art* to a larger audience.

Arati Subramanyam and Navidita Thapa have infused life into the *thaṅkas* in this book with their sensitive design.

Debasree Bhattacharjee and Dipa Chaudhuri made many useful suggestions to improve the flow of the text and I have had the pleasure of accepting these suggestions.

My gratitude to the four *Vidyapālas* who have watched over the entire effort like the four *lokapālas* of Budhism.

Our conjoined efforts to present the aesthetics of Tibetan compassion may become the purifying cause of mental dogmas, burnt by the bonfire of wisdom.

Index